In *Changed Through Faith*, I
become unstuck in life and s₁
he provide powerful steps t.... ... ., ..., ...
shows you how to put them into practice as you live each day.

-Gordon Wickert, Author & Founder, *Hope In Numbers*

If you want a how-to book to grow in your faith, this is it.
Brian's encouraging style and accessible framework for faith
development will help individuals and groups advance in their
faith and live changed lives!

-Trevor Santor, Pastor of Discipleship and Sports,
Adventure Church; Author & Founder, *Baseball Genesis*

Brian has a true passion for helping others change their lives in
positive ways and grow in their faith. Every time Brian speaks at
our Fight Club men's ministry events, our men leave inspired,
encouraged, and equipped with the next steps they need to
grow in their relationships with God. You will experience the
same results when you read Brian's book. This will be a catalyst
for change in your life!

-Rob White, Lead Pastor, *Freedom Church Cincinnati*

Brian says this: "Whether you are a dad who travels, a single
mom, a CEO, a shuttle driver, a church staff member, in college,
in business, in recovery, in prison, in the city, or on a farm, I
want to help you implement real and lasting change in your
daily life." The cool thing is that he really means it because
he's the kind of guy who truly cares about people, and God
has given him the tools to carry out the desires of his big heart.
Read this book and let the wisdom and love flow into your life.

-Cindy McDaniel, Retired Ministry Director,
Regional Consultant and Coach for *Ministry Ventures, Inc.*

We have had a front row seat to witness the amazing change in Brian's life over the past several years. He practices what he preaches, and we have seen the results of this four-step action plan in his family and the lives of others in very real ways. Turn the page and grab your front row seat to learn how to do the same!

-Tom & Jeanne Ruter, Board of Directors,
Changed Through Faith Ministries

CHANGED
THR🕆UGH
FAITH

Four Steps to **Activating** *a Life of*
PEACE, PURPOSE, *and* **FULFILLMENT**

BRIAN GOSLEE

Published by Author Academy Elite
P.O. Box 43, Powell, OH 43065
www.AuthorAcademyElite.com

Library of Congress Cataloging: 2019940625

Softcover: 978-1-64085-664-6
Hardcover: 978-1-64085-665-3
E-book: 978-1-64085-666-0

Available in softcover, hardcover, e-book, and audiobook.

DEDICATION

I dedicate this book to Brother Larry Reese, my discipleship pastor and brother in Christ. You have taught me how to be in true relationship with God my Father. You are a man of God who loves God and loves others like no one I have ever seen on this earth.

Thank you, Larry, for all you have done for me and all of God's people!

Love in Christ,

Brian

TABLE OF CONTENTS

FOREWORD

"I want to be closer to God, but I don't know how."

Many people say this—maybe, even you. *Changed Through Faith* is a powerful book that will help you walk more closely with God and grow in your faith. As you do, you will experience transformation in your life.

Brian wrote Changed Through Faith with practical how-to steps that activate change in people's lives. Brian presents these spiritual truths through down-to-earth stories and applications that connect to your everyday experiences.

Brian's heart and passion come through loudly and clearly—he wants you to experience great peace and joy by helping you activate your faith, thereby activating change in your life. His deep desire to help God's people comes from his own experience. He can teach it because he experienced it.

I believe this book should be required reading for both those who attend church and those who do not. It is an essential resource for every pastor and leader to use with those who seek to grow in their faith and relationship with God. Anyone struggling with uncertainty, anxiety, or their purpose in life will find tremendous insight and encouragement in these pages.

I urge you to read this book. As you do, be inspired to grow, take action, and follow God's ways. Like Brian, I pray you are impacted by the power and glory of God to live a life of significance that is *Changed Through Faith*.

Pat Gano
John Maxwell Trainer, Speaker, Coach
Author of *The Language of Heaven*

ACKNOWLEDGMENTS

Many people were helpful and encouraging during the writing and production of this book and are behind it as well. First, a heartfelt thank you to my wife, Andrea, and my children, Jordan and Lauren, for their support, patience, and love throughout this multi-year process. Thank you to my ministry brothers, Trevor Santor and Gordon Wickert: you guys get it and are genuine men of God! Thank you to my steadfast encouragers, ministry board members, and supporters, Dick Kent, Tom Ruter, and Charley Hartmann. I truly would not have completed this book without you! Thank you to Bill & Julie Goslee for your support and generosity. Thank you to Jeff & Hazel Bloomfield, who took a risk on me professionally and provided the Lord's provision right when it was needed. Thank you to my great friends and brothers in Christ, who always had time for me, along with a prayerful and listening ear, usually with a cup of coffee in hand: Dennis, Mike, Drews, Karl, and Tim.

Thank you to our God for choosing to move me to write this book so that others can be encouraged by His greatness. He loves you and wants you to lead a life that is genuinely *Changed Through Faith*!

Love to you all,

Brian

CHAPTER 1
TIME FOR A CHANGE

Do you feel stuck?

Do you need a change in your life?

Do you need to experience more peace and less frustration?

Do you find yourself falling into the same patterns of poor choices and making excuses for it?

Do you ever feel like there must be something more to life, like something's missing?

If you answered "yes" to any of these questions, take heart because I want you to know two things:

1. You are not alone
2. You have the right book in your hands

How do I know? Because I answered "yes" to every one of those questions, and I know you are not holding this book by accident. You are supposed to be holding it, reading it, and putting it into action. If you do, you will find answers that will turn those questions into growth and victories as you learn to experience a life *changed through faith*.

Like you and me, many people have these same questions, thoughts, and feelings. Their life is on autopilot, like mine was, lacking peace and purpose. Others are not sure how to move forward, grow in their faith, or find fulfillment.

Can you relate to this?

I was frustrated, stuck, and unfulfilled, but here's what you need to know:

1. God changed my life.
2. He can change yours too.
3. I want to help you get there, and sooner than I did.

God changed my life by moving me from being stuck to finding peace, purpose, and fulfillment. I believe He will do the same for you when you follow the four-step process in the pages that follow.

Wherever you are in life, know that encouragement and change are waiting for you.

Let's dive in a little deeper.

FRUSTRATED, STUCK, AND UNFULFILLED

I was frustrated.

With what? I engaged in the same cycles of thought and behavior that didn't yield the right results. I knew I was capable of doing better, and God was calling me to more. No matter how many drives I took to think, no matter how many times I went to church and resolved to do better, I resorted back to the same old behavior of isolating myself, engaging in secret sin, feeling ashamed, and then doing it all over again.

I was stuck.

How? My marriage and spiritual life did not improve because I didn't do anything differently, and I did not reach out to anyone else. My relationship with my spouse stalled because I did not put in any effort. I was too busy trying to escape my pain.

I comforted myself by thinking I was a great dad. Then I used that "fact" to excuse my poor choices and sin in other areas. I thought, "I know I'm not supposed to do this, but it's okay because I'm still a good dad, and it's not hurting the kids." That kept me stuck in a cycle of sinning, followed by excusing my sin.

I was stuck as a Christian because I constantly jumped in and out of God's will for me.

I was unfulfilled.

Why? I looked in the wrong places for fulfillment and relied on my own ideas to find and chase my purpose instead of pursuing an active relationship with God.

My search for joy and significance was in the job, my kids' achievements, or next big event. After a couple of years in a new job, I felt stuck and frustrated. Why? Because the newness wore off. I expected my job to provide fulfillment. I kept thinking the next great dad moment would fill me up. When those things didn't deliver more than temporary happiness, I felt stuck. I numbed the pain anyway I could, which became a vicious cycle.

I WAS DOING LIFE MY WAY

All my life, I said I was a Christian. I believed in God. I went to church. I prayed. But I did life, and Christianity, *my way*.

As a result, I found myself continually fluctuating between right and wrong behaviors, making it up as I went along. As I entered my forties, married with two children, I tried to be a *good guy* but was miserable on the inside.

I coached my son's sports teams.
I went to my daughter's sporting and academic events.
I was there for my wife—sometimes.
I tried to learn more and take steps to do the right things.
I served most Sundays at church and read the Bible sometimes.

"That's more than most people," I thought. (Beware of comparison, the great tool of the enemy!)

Doing things *my way* meant I stuffed my feelings about job challenges, financial stress, and raising kids. That resulted in emotional pain, feelings of being stuck, and a nagging sense there must be something more to life.

For many years, I numbed my frustration and pain with poor decisions, which developed into bad habits. Those bad habits, which I kept hidden in the darkness of secrecy, grew like mold into habitual sin. The habitual sins graduated to addictions.

My brain became rewired along the way, which resulted in very detrimental ways of thinking, behaving, and living. I tried to figure things out by myself. I didn't follow God in an active way, other than to go to church on Sundays and say an occasional prayer for something I wanted.

I was stuck, ashamed, and knew something was missing.

Most nights, my thought process went something like this:

> Well, it's time to unwind. Finally got the kids to bed. Yeah, I know I shouldn't do this, but I'm still a good dad and husband. I'm not hurting anyone. These things aren't hurting my job. After all, I deserve it.

However, here is the truth I ignored:

> Addicted to these areas of sin, I eroded my relationship with my spouse and destroyed my view of my worth and value, as I struggled with shame and guilt. I did not reach out to anyone else. These choices negatively affected my health and longevity. By not embracing who God said I was or moving closer to Him, I missed out on all that God had for me.

Do you identify with any of this?

Many people are worn out from trying to be a good person but still experience frustration, fear, and lack of purpose. Many people feel stuck in patterns of poor choices. Many people aren't sure how to grow spiritually or be the person God has called them to be.

That was me until God radically transformed my life.

IT WAS TIME FOR A CHANGE

On November 1, 2013, I experienced unexpected miraculous healing. It happened at a very unexpected time. I was in a doctor's office having a minor surgical procedure. While the medical staff was out of the room, I watched an interview with a former athlete who had overcome sin areas in his life, similar to mine. It was as if God was right in the room, talking directly to me.

Then, the man in the interview said something I will never forget, "To surrender is to win." Immediately, I sensed a double meaning. First, surrender the idea that I had my sin areas under control. Second, surrender to God completely.

Deeply touched, my chest pounded, and tears came to my eyes. God healed me simultaneously of two addictions that had controlled my life and thinking for over fifteen years. I walked out of that doctor's office a changed person—*changed through faith*!

That day, *I surrendered to win*. I believed in the healing and accepted it by faith with complete gratitude. The sinful habits I struggled with for so many years were destroyed and taken away instantly!

That healing was only the beginning. My transformation took place in the following months and years. I realized I searched for my joy, peace, and meaning everywhere *except in an active relationship with God*. He replaced fear with faith, frustration with joy, and anxiety with peace. Meaning and purpose for life came from its source—God.

I started living a life of active faith. I went from being a one-day-a-week Christian to a seven-days-a-week Christian. My faith developed through practical actions, like studying the Bible, worshiping God, talking with other mature Christians, and praying more frequently and boldly. As a result, I became a better dad and husband.

Since I did things *differently*, I experienced many *changes* in my life. I discovered a consistent peace and joy that eluded me for so many years.

That is what I want for you. I want to help you get there faster than I did and be supported and encouraged while you do!

YOU ARE NOT ALONE

So, let me ask again.

Do you feel stuck?

Do you want to grow in your faith in God?

Are you searching for more peace, purpose, and fulfillment in life?

Many people have these questions and feel like there must be something more to life.

There is a solution. Pursue God actively and live a life changed through faith.

I desire to help you do that, but not in a wishy-washy, pie-in-the-sky way. This book is full of faith development concepts to help you grow in your faith and relationship with God. I have intentionally included practical application and action steps.

Whether you are a dad who travels, a single mom, a CEO, a shuttle driver, a church staff member, in college, in business, in recovery, in prison, in the city, or on a farm, I want to help you implement real and lasting change in your daily life.

You will discover the solution I experienced, through an easy-to-remember, four-step action plan. By sharing the transformational stages of my faith journey as well as the stories of others, you will learn and apply this plan to your life.

Your path will not look exactly like mine or anyone else's, nor should it. Your journey is *your journey* that we will positively affect. The stages, action steps, and stories in this book will encourage you and provide real-life examples and applications to help you live a life changed through faith.

By the end of this book, you will:

1. Understand how your life can have greater peace, purpose, and fulfillment.
2. Find a sense of belonging and encouragement through reading and identifying with themes and stories of others. Learn how they overcame their struggles through a life of active faith in God.
3. Experience real change in your life through a four-step action plan.

God changed my life from one of merely existing day-to-day to a life of purpose and freedom. It happened through healing and personally *taking action.*

Don't miss this. Yes, God has the plan and the power, but you have a critical part to play. If you want to experience change, you must *take action.*

You already took your first action step by reading this book. Congratulations!

If you change your thoughts, beliefs, and actions, you will experience change in your life.

If you don't, you won't.

The truth is we all have faith in something or someone. Through our everyday activities and actions, we demonstrate what we believe in, no matter what we say.

> If you change your thoughts, beliefs, and actions, you will experience change in your life.
>
> If you don't, you won't.

Where we invest our thoughts, time, and treasure points to what we believe—money, security, parenting role, job title, another person, or God, to name a few.

It's time for a change. To experience God's peace, determine our purpose, and discover fulfillment, we must actively pursue God. That is what it means to live a life *changed through faith.*

God has a plan that can only be fulfilled *by you* through your unique gifts, talents, and obedience. Not only is your destiny dependent on it, but so are other people. By learning to live out your faith in God actively, you will be well on your way to living the life He intended for you.

Let's get started!

CHAPTER 2
THE JOURNEY

When we actively pursue God and change in our lives, we realize it's a journey of many seasons and variations—some can be dramatic and some minor. Some periods are short, while others are long.

One of the better times in my life as a dad started when my daughter was three or four years old. Every time we traveled in the car, we engaged in the same routine. This seemingly minor event began with our tan, four-door Toyota Corolla and one of those navy blue booster seats with the high back.

I struggled day-after-day to corkscrew my body around my daughter's feet as I stretched the seatbelt out all the way. Stretching my arm to maximum capacity, I blindly felt around the other side of the seat for the buckle. Without fail, the car seat had moved *on top* of the buckle. So, I was hunched over with half of my body in the backseat, pulling the seatbelt, trying not to let it retract. At the same time, I used my other hand to slide the car seat (with a toddler in it) off the top the top of the buckle, so that I could latch the seatbelt. Sometimes I would get it on the first attempt. Most often, however, my daughter would have to get out so I could adjust the position of the empty booster seat and start all over, resulting in the successful fastening of the safety belt that would protect my precious passenger.

Then one day, something akin to a miracle happened. We went out to the car; I let my daughter into the backseat where she hopped into the blue booster seat and buckled the seatbelt all by herself. I didn't have to climb in the backseat or strain my back. My daughter could now buckle her seatbelt. More importantly, we could now leave for every place five minutes later!

While this may not seem book-worthy to you, it was huge for my wife and me. (Okay, at least to me!) It represented a new season when our kids were old enough to explore activities like baseball and dance. I remember that season of life with many fond memories.

I also remember some of the tough times with my kids as teenagers. However, some of these challenging seasons ultimately became significant times of learning and growth for all of us.

What season are you in right now?

Are you in a transition? Is life stale and status quo? Or maybe it's a little too exciting or tumultuous.

Remember that life has many scenes and seasons where we exercise patience and trust in God. Remember, the story is not over.

Pastor Steven Furtick of Elevation Church put it like this,

> "Your scene is not your story. It's just one scene."
> (Furtick, S. *There's More to the Story*. Sermon. 12/5/2016)

Our faith development is a journey, too. It has many different scenes and seasons. Read any story of any character in the Bible, and you will find there are ups and downs, joys and sorrows, periods of great struggle, and times of great blessing. Why would we think our lives and experience with God would be any different?

JOSEPH, THE SON OF JACOB

Consider the story of Joseph, son of Jacob, from the book of Genesis (chapters 37-50).

When Joseph was a teenager, his brothers became jealous of him, threw him into an empty well, then sold him into slavery. As if that were not bad enough, while he was a slave, he resisted the temptation to have an affair with Potiphar's wife. Accused anyway, Potiphar wrongly threw him in prison. While in prison, he faithfully interpreted some dreams for his fellow prisoners. Two years later, Pharaoh called for Joseph to interpret some dreams for him. As a result of this interaction and its impact, Joseph was made second-in-command over all of Egypt. Later, during a seven-year famine, his brothers ended up on his doorstep. He showed mercy and compassion and eventually brought his whole family to live in a new land.

Joseph's story is one of obedience. However, this often did not result in what we would consider blessings. He had many unexpected low points in his life. Even though he followed

God in faith, he still went from being a slave to becoming a prisoner! Despite that, he eventually arrived in the ultimate position and appointment God had for him.

By the end of his journey, God's purposes and provision prevailed for not only Joseph but also his entire family. Joseph could never have seen any of this coming when he was with his brothers, in the pit, thrown in jail, or even appointed to power. Only when reunited with his family did the full revelation of God's plan occur.

> God has sent me [Joseph] ahead of you to keep you and your families alive and to preserve many survivors. So it was God who sent me [Joseph] here, not you [his brothers]! And he is the one who made me an advisor to Pharaoh—the manager of his entire palace and the governor of all Egypt.
>
> (Genesis 45:7–8 NLT)

Joseph's story illustrates how God has a great purpose and plan for each of us, but how we often cannot fully see it along the way.

I know this has been true for me. There have been many twists and turns in my journey. Like Joseph, I didn't realize it along the way, but God took me through an action plan to change me and my life.

CHAPTER 3
THE ACTION PLAN

Reflecting on my journey, God revealed four distinct action steps I want to teach you so you can experience a fulfilling life changed through faith. They are easy to remember and say. Read these four steps out loud right now:

1. BELIEVE
2. RECEIVE
3. LIVE IT
4. GIVE IT

BELIEVE

The boldness of our belief helps us forge ahead, in spite of any doubt or fear.

Believe that God is who He says He is, has a great plan for each of us, and delivers on His promises. It doesn't mean we don't have doubt, but the boldness of our belief helps us forge ahead, in spite of any doubt or fear.

RECEIVE

As we *believe* in faith, we *receive* God in our hearts and all He offers to us. It is one thing to believe, but another to receive, which is an important part of our relationship and experience with God. It takes time.

LIVE IT

While our hearts and minds must focus on God, ultimately, we need to *live it* out daily to experience real change in our lives and the lives of others. We need to put our faith into action.

GIVE IT

All of this is not only for our growth and benefit; it is for others. God wants us to live a life of generosity with our time, talents, treasures, compassion, and Christ-like love.

Initially, these four steps in our faith development are progressive. However, as we mature in our faith, we find that they do not necessarily happen in sequence. In fact, on most days, you experience all four steps, in no particular order.

In the following chapters, I unpack each step to live a life full of peace, purpose, and meaning. Through stories, illustrations, and practical application tips, you will experience the motivation, encouragement, and support you need to pursue a life of active faith in God.

If you implement this plan, expect a transformation in:

(1) You
(2) Your life

ILLUSTRATION — PART ONE

Visual illustrations help us remember things. As I wrote this book, I believed that an illustration was important to have for the four steps of this faith development action plan. I tried to think of something that was simple and effective, but nothing seemed right.

Sometimes you obey God even though you don't feel like it. While driving to see someone I thought God wanted me to visit (I didn't have the time or desire to go on this particular day), I got an idea for the illustration, along with its meaning.

God often helps us and provides direction when we are least expecting it but are obeying Him. It is not according to our timing but His. I'm grateful for the illustration because it helps us visualize these concepts.

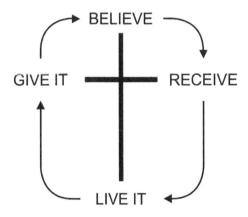

Let's review the illustration: Through faith, we BELIEVE in God and His plans for us, we RECEIVE blessings, love, and forgiveness, LIVE it out every day, and GIVE it away by serving and loving others.

ILLUSTRATION — PART TWO

Reviewing this illustration further, put a person (you) in it. When we do that, we notice some interesting things:

- Believe is at the head of the diagram, where your mind is
- Receive is in your left hand, where you receive a gift
- Live is at your feet, where you walk out your faith in action daily
- Give is at your right hand, where you greet others with a handshake or give generously
- Most importantly, your heart is at the intersection point

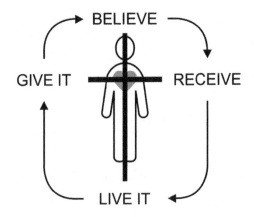

Later, you will read about the importance of the "facing of our hearts." Our hearts need to be open and facing God, or even great intentions will not have God-sized results. For example, if we consider a great mission idea, but our hearts are wrong, we don't serve God in the way He intends. If we live out our faith with our feet by serving at church or giving our resources, but our hearts are not right, we don't accomplish God's purposes.

Let's review the illustration from a more personal perspective.

BELIEVE

What do you believe about yourself? Is it positive or negative? What do you believe about God? Is it positive or negative?

Wherever you are in life, God wants you to believe and have faith in Him. The *old me* had negative beliefs about myself and negative thoughts about God. The *new me* has positive beliefs about myself and positive thoughts about God.

> *Do not lie to one another, seeing that you have put off the old self with its practices and have put on the new self, which is being renewed in knowledge after the image of its creator.*
>
> (Colossians 3:9-10 ESV)

Believing with your mind means that you **make a decision**. God doesn't want us to leave our brains out of our journeys of faith. He wants us to use our minds as we follow Him. He wants to help us think more like Him. We need to believe and trust in who God is and decide to put Him first in our lives through a relationship with Jesus Christ.

Here is a story Jesus told about belief, as recorded in the Bible by John, a close disciple of Jesus.

> *Eight days later, his disciples were inside again, and Thomas was with them. Although the doors were locked, Jesus came and stood among them and said, "Peace be with you." Then he said to Thomas, "Put your finger here, and see my hands; and put out your hand, and place it in my side. Do not disbelieve, but **believe**." Thomas answered him, "My Lord and my God!" Jesus said to him, "Have you **believed** because you have seen me? Blessed are those who have not seen and yet have **believed**."*

Now Jesus did many other signs in the presence of the disciples,
which are not written in this book; but these are written so that
*you may **believe** that Jesus is the Christ, the Son of God, and that*
*by **believing** you may have life in his name. (emphasis added)*

(John 20:26-31 ESV)

Jesus also put it this way:

"For God so loved the world, that he gave his only Son, that
whoever believes in him should not perish but have eternal life."

(John 3:16 ESV)

Make the decision every day to believe in God for who He is, and
put Him first in your life. It may take time, but you can learn.

RECEIVE

Think about the last time you gave someone a gift on their
birthday or at Christmas. What happened when you offered
it to them? They reached out with open hands to receive it.
(And, hopefully, they liked it!)

Now picture your arms stretched out with your left hand open
to receive a gift. Picture God, placing love, forgiveness, and
wisdom into your open left hand. If your hand is closed in a fist because you are angry or resistant, you cannot receive the gifts. To receive the blessings, have an *open hand, open heart* approach to God.

> To receive the blessings, have an *open hand, open heart* approach to God.

We *receive* God's love, forgiveness, peace, joy, and other gifts and share them by living our faith and giving to others.

LIVE IT

Live is at the foot of the cross diagram. Metaphorically and literally, we use our feet to get where God wants us to go.

When you walk, what happens? You are active as you use your legs and feet to move from one place to another. As my mom advanced in age, the doctor's number one piece of advice to her was, "Get up and walk. Be active."

I have friends who are not able to walk. I have a physical condition that causes a limp and frequent pain when walking. When we have trouble walking, others can use their feet to help us get to where we need to go. Jesus was the same way. He walked thousands of miles during His time on earth, actively living out His beliefs and purpose.

Living a life of active faith is the key area where I want to help you. I will bring it up again and again. Why? Because I believe actively living out our faith, seven days a week is the key to experiencing all that God has for us in this life and eternal life. After all, as a Christian, I *believed* in God for many years and even *received* His forgiveness and restoration in many ways. However, on many days, I was miserable and struggled in my life and faith. It was not until I began to *live it* and *give it* that my life became *changed through faith*.

This theme emerges in the stories contained in this book, both those in the Bible and those living today: Until people started *living out their faith actively,* they didn't experience real transformation in their lives and the full impact of their purpose.

If we believe and receive God, but don't live it out and give it away to others, we are limiting our experience in life and what God can accomplish for others through us.

> For as the body apart from the spirit is dead, so also faith apart from works is dead.
>
> (James 2:26 ESV)

GIVE IT

Remember when I asked you to picture yourself giving someone a gift? Let's do that again.

What do you see as you give the gift? You see the other person stretch out their arms and hands in anticipation. Often, you see a smile. When they open it, you may hear a gasp of joy or receive a hug of thanks.

Growing in our faith is awesome. It is wonderful to walk closely with God! However, this is not only for our benefit. At some point, we need to realize, "It's not about me." As we grow and become *changed through faith*, we develop a greater capacity to serve others, love them, and help them discover God is active in their lives.

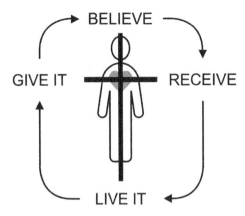

We receive from the Lord in one hand. When that gift passes along the horizontal axis, through a heart that is receptive and focused on Him, we use our other hand to *give* away God's love in many different ways.

*   *   *

These areas of responding to God are from my experience, yet I see these same areas at work in other people's lives. I hope you learn and remember how to *believe, receive, live,* and *give* your faith and love of Jesus Christ in your way.

Remember, everyone's experience is unique. You don't have to be like anyone else. God designed you uniquely, and your journey is made especially for you. Embrace that!

One day, I put in in my journal this way:

> Walk in full confidence and calmness that can only come from God. I don't have to be like ANYONE else except for Him. Jesus is my example. (Personal journal, April 28, 2015)

God has a destiny for you and me. I still blow it; I still miss the mark. We all do. Nevertheless, I do not miss the mark quite as often. I experience peace, joy, and God's healing power more consistently. I love God and others more every day. That's what I want for you, too!

We choose the destiny we experience by how we activate our faith.

We choose the destiny we experience by how we activate our faith. God has a calling for you, which is yours alone. He is waiting for you to walk into it. Not only that, but others are waiting, too!

As we embark on this four-part plan, here are some questions to consider:

> How long will you try and figure things out on your own?

> How long will you stay frustrated?

> How long will you put your focus and faith in things of this world, only to repeatedly think, "Something is missing in my life"?

I've been there. For thirty years, that was my life! You can get to a better place in your spiritual journey much sooner than I did.

Are you ready to walk into a life of greater peace, purpose, and fulfillment?

Let's get started with the first step of the plan: *Believe.*

CHAPTER 4
BELIEVE

And without faith it is impossible to please him, for whoever would draw near to God must believe that he exists and that he rewards those who seek him.

(Hebrews 11:6 ESV)

WHY START WITH BELIEF?

Simple. *Your actions are products of your beliefs.*

Here are some examples:

➤ If I believe I need money to eat and a job provides the funds, I get a job.

➤ If I believe my children need organization, rules, and structure to grow up properly, I supply it.

➢ If I believe the seatbelt in my car will protect me, I buckle it.

You can tell me what you believe, but ultimately you will *show me your beliefs* by your actions. So, it is important that our belief system is intact and aligned. What do I mean by aligned? As a Christian, "in alignment" means in agreement with God, His Word, and my relationship with God through Jesus Christ.

WHAT IS BELIEF?

According to the dictionary, belief is "an acceptance that a statement is true or that something exists." (Oxford Dictionaries Online, s.v. "belief," accessed March 27, 2019. https://en.oxforddictionaries.com/definition/belief.)

Here are some examples:

➢ I believe my car is safe.

➢ I believe my spouse is a good person.

➢ I believe in God.

To go a layer deeper, the second dictionary definition of belief is "trust, faith, or confidence in someone or something." (Oxford Dictionaries Online, s.v. "belief," accessed March 27, 2019. https://en.oxforddictionaries.com/definition/belief.)

➢ I believe (have confidence) that the brakes will stop my car when I press the brake pedal.

➢ I believe (trust) that my spouse will love me for the long term.

> ➢ I believe (trust, have faith in, have confidence in) the existence of God as Creator of this world, and believe He exists as Father, Son, and Holy Spirit.

Having belief doesn't mean we can always see what we believe. I do not see my brake pads when I apply the brake pedal. However, I feel the effects of it acting on my belief, and it builds my confidence for the next time.

I may not observe my spouse making an actual decision to love me every single day, but I trust that she is faithful to her vows. I learn her character over time and believe since she has loved me before, she will continue to love me.

It is one thing to *believe*, but it is another to *receive* it and *live it* out. We will cover those concepts in the following chapters.

LEARNING FROM THE CHILDREN

Jesus told his disciples to become like children.

> *And he said: "Truly I tell you, unless you change and become like little children, you will never enter the kingdom of heaven."*
>
> (Matthew 18:3 NIV)

Let's look at this example from a child I know.

My friend, Tony, and his wife Jennifer have an eighteen-month-old, adorable son named Joey. I see Joey and his parents every six to twelve months. Two visits ago, he was crawling. The last time I visited, he was walking. What? How did that happen so fast? It was great seeing him advance in his growth and cruise around!

When Joey started walking, some part of his brain had to believe he could walk. Some part of his mind had to trust that if he put one foot in front of the other, he would stay upright and get to his destination. He had to put into action what he learned from watching his parents.

Joey now walks around the house and the backyard, chasing squirrels and colorful playground balls. He does this with a permanent smile on his face, while Tony and Jennifer watch, and sometimes follow close behind!

Like Joey, we take an initial step of belief in God. Then, every day, we choose to believe and trust in Jesus and practice walking with Him as our leader. As Joey learned to walk from watching his parents, we learn to walk in faith by observing how Jesus and others do it.

Like Tony and Jennifer pick up Joey when he falls, our Father is there to pick us up every time we fall. As Joey grows up, he will believe his mom and dad are there for him. He will make decisions about his beliefs. Likewise, as we grow in our faith, we understand from experience that God our Father is there for us.

If we believe in our relationship with God, we will have experiences that go with that belief. We must practice walking with belief as Joey does. When we do, the joy in our hearts mirrors the smile on Joey's face.

ACTIVE BELIEF IN GOD

Ultimately, our most fundamental step of active faith is a complete belief that God exists, and is who He says. This belief is not a surface level acceptance, but rather confidence and trust that is deep in your heart. Believe in God as the Creator of heaven and earth. Have faith that God is Father, Son, and Holy Spirit.

When Jesus healed people, He often said, "Your faith has made you well." He didn't say, "I healed you." He didn't say, "All those good deeds tipped the scales in your favor, my man, you're healed!" He didn't say, "It looks like you were in the right place at the right time, so get up and walk!" He said their *faith* or *belief* healed them. They believed Jesus could heal them.

> Jesus stopped and ordered the man to be brought to him. When he came near, Jesus asked him, "What do you want me to do for you?"
>
> "Lord, I want to see," he replied.
>
> Jesus said to him, "Receive your sight; your faith has healed you." Immediately he received his sight and followed Jesus, praising God. When all the people saw it, they also praised God.
>
> (Luke 18:40-43 NIV)

FAITH AS CONVICTION

A personal relationship with God starts with belief, with faith. This faith is more than simple acceptance of God or that a great man named Jesus walked the earth; it's deeper than that. Faith in God doesn't need to be complicated, but it does need to become deep and convicted because it will be tested.

Faith means having *conviction.* According to vocabulary.com, conviction is "an unshakable belief in something without need for proof or evidence." ("Conviction–Dictionary Definition." Vocabulary.com, accessed March 27, 2019. https://www.vocabulary.com/dictionary/conviction.)

For example, I have a conviction that telling the truth is extremely important. What is one you have? That unshakable belief is more than something you "kind of believe." It connects to your values, behaviors, and decisions.

Faith in God is not a surface level concept that we "kind of believe there's a God" when someone asks us. Instead, faith includes a deep-down conviction that God exists. We must believe in our hearts and minds that Jesus is the Son of God, who walked this earth, died, and three days later rose from the grave and conquered sin and death—overcame it—destroyed it!

> *For everyone who has been born of God overcomes the world.*
> *And this is the victory that has overcome the world—our faith.*
>
> *(1 John 5:4 ESV)*

BELIEF AND TRUST

When you believe someone, you trust them to:

- Be there for you
- Remain loyal and faithful
- Follow through on their promises

You trust them in good times and in bad. When you believe someone, you also believe *in* them.

We can believe *in* God for these same attributes. He is a loyal, faithful, promise-keeper, who is always with us. Don't merely believe there *is* a God; believe *in* God for who He is. Believe He wants to build and ignite these same qualities in you! After all, He made you in His image.

> Believe *in* God for who He is. Believe He wants to build and ignite these same qualities in you!

ANDREA GOSLEE— WIFE, MOTHER, MINISTRY DIRECTOR

Speaking of people whom I believe and trust, after God, my wife is at the top of that list. God places specific people strategically in our lives, which definitely is the case with my wife.

Andrea exhibits belief and faith like no one else I know. She's believed in me for thirty years, even when the evidence said, "You're wrong. He's a knucklehead!"

She believes in God; therefore, she believes in me. She sees what God has done in lives all around her, including hers and mine. She has experienced God moving mountains in our life, and she believes He will do it again.

For the entire twenty-seven years of our marriage, she has been in church ministry. Her dedication to helping children and their families encounter Jesus and walk with Him has been remarkable.

Along with leading a vibrant and exemplary children's ministry, she is an amazing wife and mother. When our kids were young, she stayed home and poured into them, while still leading church ministry. She does everything with a humble, loving, kind heart and an active spirit, never wavering in her faith and dependence on God.

What does this active spirit look like?

When she wanted to shout at me for my bad choices, she prayed and treated me with love and patience instead.

When our son was born nearly three months premature, she believed in God with an uncommon and uncanny calmness throughout the emergency delivery and subsequent twelve weeks that he was in NICU. He weighed 2 lbs. 11 oz. Andrea never felt alarmed or scared. She believed in her great big God with a calmness that only came from Him. I am happy to report that our son is now a healthy college student and a great young man!

When I freaked out about a job change or a difficult situation with our kids, she remained calm and believed God would work it out. And He did—every time.

Her belief, her faith in God, is active and strong every day—a tremendous example to our family and those around her.

I am incredibly grateful God blessed me with a wife who waited patiently for her knuckleheaded husband to finally come around. All the while, she has set a remarkable example of patience and consistent joy in the Lord, impacting her family and thousands of children and their families for Christ. Andrea has an active faith in God and lives it out daily.

BIBLICAL EXAMPLE OF BELIEF—A FATHER & CHILD

I love the way Jesus describes the power of belief and faith in this story from the Gospel of Mark. Listen to this father who brings his son to Jesus for healing:

> And Jesus asked his father, "How long has this been happening to Him?" And He said, "From childhood. And it has often cast him into the fire and into water, to destroy him. But if you can do anything, have compassion on us and help us." And Jesus said to him, " 'If you can'! All things are possible for one who believes." Immediately the father of the child cried out and said, "I believe; help my unbelief!" And when Jesus saw that a crowd came running together, he rebuked the unclean spirit, saying to it, "You mute and deaf spirit, I command you, come out of him and never enter him again."
>
> (Mark 9:21-25 ESV)

Jesus says, "If I can?" I see a bit of humor in this. Consider this in more contemporary terms. It's as if Jesus says, "If I can? C'mon man, I'm Jesus. God in the flesh, right here on earth. You wouldn't ask Tom Brady if he 'can' throw a touchdown pass, would you?"

But Jesus has none of the ego or bravado I described. He doesn't claim that He heals. Instead, He declares that *belief* is the essential ingredient to healing: "*All things are possible for one who believes.*" We respond to God in faith, and God responds to our faith.

Throughout the gospel accounts of Jesus' life, He frequently teaches about belief in all types of environments: traveling with His disciples, teaching the crowds, communicating with individuals, and praying.

On one occasion, while teaching a crowd, Jesus said,

> *"For this is the will of my Father, that everyone who looks on the Son and believes in Him should have eternal life."*
>
> *(John 6:40 ESV)*

Believing is mostly about what is in your mind, soul, and heart. God wants you to use your *mind* in your faith, not only your heart or emotions. You can't see some of the *believe* stage, because it is in your mind and your heart. Nevertheless, the way you live out your life, as well as where you spend your time and resources, speak volumes about what you believe.

If you *believe* God is who He says He is; if you *believe* He is Father, Son, and Holy Spirit; if you *believe* He delivers on His promises, then the way you live your life *changes*. Here are some examples of what that change could look like:

> ➤ You do not spend as much time chasing the things of this world.

> ➤ You do not sacrifice family time in the name of being the provider.

> ➤ You do not gossip about others to feel better about yourself and your shortcomings.

> ➤ You do not constantly think about where and when you will get your next drink or drug.

I give these examples to encourage, not criticize or judge. I did many of these things, but because I now *believe* differently, I *behave* differently. Because my beliefs are more aligned with God, I experience freedom from those former motivations for my decisions and actions. Did I do all this by myself? Of course not. We will learn more when we discuss receiving from God and living out our faith.

These are practical examples from my life to show how your life could change on the outside, based on beliefs you hold on the inside. You live out your beliefs.

Pastor Steven Furtick from Elevation Church (North Carolina) said it this way:

> "Your faith will always follow your focus. Whatever you're most focused on, you will have the most faith in."
> (Furtick, S. *Functional Faith*. Sermon. April 10, 2016)

In short, when you believe deeply in God and all that He is, you consistently *"Set your mind on things that are above, not on things that are on the earth"* (Colossians 3:2 ESV).

CASE STUDY IN BELIEF—RANDY

A Life Changed Through Faith

> "Don't be afraid to cry out." - Randy

Randy's story speaks of amazing healing from addiction and a desperate belief in God. It is also a realistic story to encourage you, no matter your circumstances, to hang in there and know it is a process.

Randy learned about and trusted in God, even when the healing didn't come. His faith resulted in a life now changed through faith! I had a chance to interview Randy about his story.

> My name is Randy, and I'm a grateful believer. I'm a father and a husband.
>
> There was a period where there was the agnostic Randy, who didn't know anything about God or Jesus and didn't think anyone else did either. I felt it was all a bunch of fluff and hooey.
>
> During that period, I was driven by what the world teaches you to be driven by—power, influence, money, cars, houses, vacations. That's how I was driven. By some accounts, I was doing pretty good at that, but I was not satisfied. I started down a path of parties and heavy drinking that led me to cocaine, which completely consumed me very quickly. So, that path went on for about seven years.
>
> The first six years, I thought, "Hey, this is a good time." I thought I was a good cocaine addict. I still had my job; I was still buying cars and still going on vacations with the family, but I was a slave to cocaine even through that. I thought I was good at it, but the last year, it had become pain and agony. I was spending three and four nights at a time in a hotel room

snorting cocaine. I did not sleep or eat; I just snorted cocaine. I would walk away from my family at any given time; I would just be gone. That went on for a year. I realized what I was doing was painful. I knew it was wrong, but I could not stop.

This new church opened up in the neighborhood, close to us. In fact, the pastor moved in right next door, which many people told me was a clear sign that God was in pursuit of me. I was still kind of leery about that, but I started to have conversations with this pastor. He started to put a little change in my heart about Christ and church and that sort of thing. I actually began to pursue more knowledge about God and a lot of it through this pastor neighbor of mine. The more I got into it, the more it made sense to me.

I started by saying to myself, "Alright, I'm going to pretend there is a God." I thought, "I'll see how that goes. I'll pretend." So, I would talk to this pretend God. In one particular case, He responded emphatically. I asked Him about a plan I had. It was a bad plan, but I thought it was a good plan at the time. Looking back, it was a very bad plan, and He explained to me that it was a bad plan and why. And I remember being so grateful for someone to be so truthful and right to the point. You'd think that would have been enough for me to say, "Oh, geez, I surrender, I'm yours." It was truthful. It was to the point.

It was right on, and there was no way it was anything else but God. I still kept using and binging, but now I knew He was real. He was there, and now I was in pursuit. I was looking for the button to push, and then He could fix all this.

I actually got to the point where I said, "Okay, this is the answer. Jesus is it. I can work with this." I started to volunteer at the church on the tech team. I would go to two services if I could. I was going to a 6:30 a.m. Bible study, Celebrate Recovery meetings, and AA meetings. I was going to make this work.

But it really wasn't changing anything.

I was doing all that, and I was gaining knowledge about Jesus, but I continued to binge. In fact, it was getting worse. The binges were becoming longer, and, financially, we were going down the tubes very fast. The creditors, the IRS, they were all calling, beating on my head, but I ignored it and kept going.

It was a very specific moment, it was April 29, 2010, around 7:30 a.m., coming out of a 6:30 a.m. Bible study meeting, and I cried out to God saying, "Hey, can I be your cocaine addict?"

I didn't think that there was any other way. I had done everything I could possibly do to get cleaned up for Jesus, and I could not do it. It wasn't possible.

His answer was pretty immediate; I immediately had no desire to do cocaine. I had curled up in my car and thought I was going to die, physically. God's plan was different. I died, yeah, emotionally, spiritually, something died, and I was born some other guy! I could tell. I immediately knew that the guy sitting in this chair had perked up, got out of the fetal position, looked up and thought, "what's going on?" I was somebody else in many, many ways—very, very different. It was immediate. I had a thirst for reading the Bible. I wanted to go to meetings and share and be part of it with other people. That was not the Randy who opened that door and got in the car. Someone else got out. I was weary when I got in the car at the point of thinking I was dying. As soon as I asked Him to be His cocaine addict, I had a burst of energy. I jumped up in my seat. I was looking around, trying to figure out, "Who did that? Where'd they go?"

There are days when I am so in love and feeling God and walking in the Holy Spirit. Then there are other days when it doesn't quite feel like that, but I know what to do now. Before, I ran somewhere. Now, I know to keep the Lord close even if I don't feel like it. I'm just being honest. There are days when I'm feeling something's not going right or whatever. Maybe I don't feel like listening to Christian radio and singing and dancing in my car like I do on other days, but I know how to keep Him close. I talk to Him even if I don't feel like it, because I know He's always going to be there. Whatever is troubling me will fade, and I can get back to just loving and smiling and singing with Jesus.

Maybe that sounds kind of weird or phony. I say that because as a previous agnostic, I would have thought that. I wouldn't have believed it. Now I experience it. I do it, and it's so real.

If you're early on and you're thinking, "I know something's got to change," you are 110% right. If you've figured out something's got to change, go after that. But the real focus behind all of that is getting close to God and getting to know Him. It is about getting to know Him and inter-acting with Him,

> If you've figured out something's got to change, go after that. But the real focus behind all of that is getting close to God and getting to know Him.

and it becomes a relationship. That comes by surrendering to Him. It really isn't doing anything on your own. I tried very hard, but that was not going to happen. Surrendering, crying out, that's it. Surrendering can look different for everyone. It doesn't have to be that you're on your deathbed crying out, but it's got to be pretty close to something like that. Don't be afraid to cry out.

APPLYING YOUR BELIEF TO A RELATIONSHIP WITH GOD

Randy demonstrated that simply learning about God wasn't enough. He needed to cry out to Him, depend on God entirely, and have a relationship with Him.

To have a relationship with God, we need to repent and receive forgiveness. Because we sin, we cannot be in right relationship with God by ourselves, without Jesus. That is why we need to accept Jesus as our Savior and follow Him. Jesus saved us from our sin and made it possible for each of us to have a relationship with God. The only way to have a right relationship with God is through Jesus Christ.

> Jesus said to him, "I am the way, and the truth, and the life. No one comes to the Father except through me."
>
> (John 14:6 ESV)

It starts with admitting we are sinners in need of a savior. Next, we need to believe that our savior is Jesus Christ, who is the risen Son of God. We then choose to repent, believe, and follow Him as the leader of our life for the rest of our days.

DO YOU NEED TO DECIDE TO BELIEVE?

To know someone, you spend time with them and build a relationship with them. That is what God wants. God wants to have a relationship with you.

If you have not yet accepted Jesus Christ as the Savior of your life, I invite you to do so right now. Turn to the resources on pg 157 for specific help.

If you do believe in God and are already a follower of Jesus, are you firm in your beliefs? Are you living them out? Do you need to recommit to your decision? Turn to the resources on pg 158 for specific help.

Finally, if you are a follower of Jesus and solid in your faith in God, I encourage you to continue growing in your faith and sharing it with others!

Believing God for who He is, accepting Jesus as your Savior, and trusting God with your life are all components of the *Believe* stage in the action plan. Once we establish a deep-seated conviction and belief in God, we *receive* Him and all He has to offer. We look at that in the next chapter.

*   *   *

It is vital to have real examples and application of these concepts to everyday life. There are practical applications to each stage of your journey in the sections entitled *Activate Your Faith* to help you be active consistently in your faith in God. These action steps are a small sample of the many practical steps included in our online programs and small group experiences. You don't need to do all of the end-of-chapter activities at once. Pick a few that resonate with you and focus on those first.

 ACTIVATE YOUR FAITH-BELIEVE

BELIEVE

Believe that God is who He says He is, has a great plan for each of us, and delivers on His promises. It doesn't mean we don't have doubt, but the boldness of our belief helps us forge ahead, in spite of any doubt or fear.

BELIEVE THROUGH PRAYER

Start each day with the prayer below, or a similar prayer of belief, surrender, and praise. (Suggestion: Post it somewhere you will see it, like your closet wall, bedroom wall, refrigerator, etc.)

> Lord, I pray as the man who brought his son to you for healing, "I believe; help my unbelief!" I believe you are the all-powerful, all-knowing, all-loving Creator of the universe and the Lord of my life. I believe in your Word.

I believe in you as Father, Son, and Holy Spirit. I believe that Jesus is the way, the truth, and the life. I repent of my sinful ways and accept Jesus as my Savior every day. Through Jesus, I believe I have a personal relationship with God and am His fully-adopted son or daughter. Help me walk forth boldly in this belief every day. Amen.

BELIEVE THROUGH THE BIBLE

Read the Bible passage below from the book of Romans. Insert your name into the blanks in these verses (in place of the name Abraham). Make it personal. Read it every day for a week, memorize it, pray it back to God, and make it your goal to believe as Abraham did.

_____ *never wavered in believing God's promise.*

In fact, [his/her] faith grew stronger, and in this [he/she] brought glory to God.

_____ *was fully convinced that God is able to do whatever He promises.*

And because of _____ *'s faith, God counted [him/her] as righteous."*

(adapted from Romans 4:20-22 NLT)

☐ **Bible Tip:** Start a regular Bible reading plan. Try the plans on the YouVersion or Changed Through Faith mobile apps. I recommend one chapter a day. Many plans last three to five days. Try searching for the keywords "Building Your Faith."

BELIEVE THROUGH RELATIONSHIPS

Look at the list of action steps below. Check any of these that you currently do (if none apply yet, that is fine). Start working toward a new one in the next two weeks. You don't have to do everything at once, but you will experience growth in your belief in God as you move through them all.

☐ I meet regularly (i.e., once per week, twice per month, etc.) with a person in my life that is a genuine Christian whom I consider to be more mature in their spiritual journey.

☐ I have joined a Christian-based or Bible-based small group (in person or online) that meets regularly.

☐ I have shared with someone in my family my new journey through this book, the desire to build my faith in God and be more active in it.

BELIEVE THROUGH A RENEWED MIND

Gratitude List

Our focus shapes our thoughts, and our thoughts shape our behavior. Having an attitude of gratitude makes a significant impact on how we approach God and life. Make a list of things for which you are grateful and post it where you will see it every day. Give God thanks for these things every day.

✓ _____

✓ _____

✓ _____

✓ _____

Look for God's power, influence, and provision. If you look for it, you will see it. Be aware and ready for evidence of God at all times. We find what we look for.

List of Answered Prayers

Start a separate list of the ways you see God at work in your life or the lives of those around you. Consider this a list of answered prayers. Even if there is nothing on it yet, have faith and *believe* it will grow. As you see God at work, add to it. As you pray and see prayers answered, add to it. Share these answered prayers with others. It will build their belief too!

✓ _____

✓ _____

✓ _____

✓ _____

BELIEVE: JOURNAL TIME

Placing Our Faith Actively in God

Reflect honestly on where you place your faith. Examine and write down in your journal three to five main areas where you spend your discretionary time and income.

Our behavior and choices demonstrate where we put our faith. Do you actively place your belief and faith in God?

Here are some questions to consider. Is my faith in:

- My agenda or God's?
- God or my comfort?
- God or my circumstances?

- God or my money?
- God or my career?

To place our faith in God means we need to spend time getting to know Him through the Bible, prayer, and community. Faith in God builds over time, which helps us give thanks in the good times and the bad, and weather the storms of life.

Do you want guidance and encouragement to complete these steps? Join an online small group, take the Changed Through Faith Action Plan course, or sign up for faith development coaching at ctfaith.com.

Next, let's learn how our relationship with God can go from *Believing* to *Receiving*.

CHAPTER 5
RECEIVE

But to all who did receive him, who believed in his name, he gave the right to become children of God.

(John 1:12 ESV)

WHY DO WE NEED TO RECEIVE?

Once our belief in God is firm, we continue our journey by growing in our relationship with Him. Receiving is an essential part of building a relationship.

Seems backward, right? After all, the famous saying from the prayer of Saint Francis of Assisi says, "It is in giving that we receive." However, in the context of our faith journey with God, we need to *receive* before we can fully live it and give it.

Why?

We can't live out our faith if we don't know and experience what it means. It's hard to give to others what you do not have. First, we receive God's love, healing, and transformation in our lives, which can take time, as in any relationship.

Let me put it this way. When you develop a relationship, you get to know the other person by listening to and learning about them—what they like, dislike, and how you can "do life" together. This process often involves you changing your ways, being more understanding, or even healing from a past relationship.

In our relationship with God, we need to learn about Him. We also need to learn from Him through an active relationship with Him. We can receive knowledge and wisdom from Him, about Him, and about ourselves, as His son or daughter. We may need to experience some healing, growth, and encouragement.

How does this change happen? It happens in many ways—prayer, studying the Bible, going to church, worshipping, talking with other believers, and listening.

How do you receive encouragement from someone? How do you collect advice from someone? How do you build a relationship with someone?

You listen—willingly.

RECEIVE BY LISTENING

Robby, my former boss, and friend was a national sales leader in his field and a great relationship builder. He shared this advice during an interview related to his industry:

> I know it's been a successful lunch if we get
> finished eating, and my plate's empty and
> theirs isn't, because they've been doing all the
> talking. If I've been doing all the talking, then
> my plate isn't touched. That isn't a good way
> to build trust. You have to care, and you have
> to care deeply.

Robby knew the way to strengthen a relationship and build trust was to listen. And you can't listen if you do all the talking or fail to spend time with the other person.

Not only is it important to receive through listening, but we need to do so *willingly*. If we are only performing a duty by listening, eagerly waiting for our chance to jump in and make our point, put up a defense, or prove the other person wrong, this will not teach us anything or strengthen the relationship. As Robby said, "You have to care, and you have to care deeply."

Have you ever listened out of duty, only waiting to tell your spouse or kid the *right way* (i.e., your way) to think or do something? I know I have. However, a healthy relationship is built on mutual trust, respect, listening, and receiving.

Here is another practical example of what a listening posture looks like, and can result in, from my life as a dad.

One night, my teenage son and I were in his room having an emotionally charged conversation. It revolved around a difference of opinion about the way he saw a social situation in his life and the way his mother and I saw it. On this occasion, instead of ramming my point home repeatedly, I decided to close my mouth and listen—really listen. I intentionally chose to actively listen to him, as opposed to taking a breath to reload with a barrage of why I was right. He explained how he felt and made his case.

Then, I took a giant leap of faith and related something I don't think I ever told him before. I took a breath, leaned back against the wall in his bedroom, and said, "You're right."

He looked at me from his bed, mouth opened, and speechless. Because I listened, that moment built trust in our relationship.

Think about your best friend, your spouse, your child. You care deeply about them. Therefore, you listen to them actively. You receive information, advice, and encouragement from them, and you give the same in return.

Our relationship with God is the same way. God cares deeply about you! He wants you to care the same way about Him. God wants to listen to you, and He wants you to listen to and receive from Him.

HOW DO WE LISTEN TO GOD?

First, our relationship with God will grow over time. We learn to listen to Him, learn more about Him, and how to walk more in alignment with Him.

Second, our minds and hearts have to be in a posture to listen to God. In short, we must set our selfish focus aside, humble ourselves, and release and repent of things in the way of effective communication in our relationship with God. If we focus only on what we want, it doesn't work well.

Think about your other relationships. If they are *all about you* and everything going your way, you're heading for troubled waters. It's the same with God. When you pray, are you trying to get God to help you with *your* agenda, or are you willing to listen and *submit to His plan* for you?

Does this mean you must be all cleaned up before you hear from God? No.

> When you pray, are you trying to get God to help you with *your* agenda, or are you willing to listen and *submit to His plan* for you?

Does this mean every time you pray specifically to hear from God, you will? No.

Does this mean you have to light votive candles, read the book of Leviticus, close the shades, and play worship music at the right volume before you can pray and hear from God? You can if you want to, but no.

Does it mean God will help you if you practice listening to Him faithfully and consistently over time? Yes.

LISTENING PRAYER

One of the best tips I ever received was from my good friend Tim. Tim is someone I mentored as he went through a difficult time in his life. Because he ran to God in his struggle, not away from Him, he came out the other side closer to God.

Even though I mentored him, Tim helped me. When you serve someone, often you receive a greater blessing in return.

Tim explained that after he does his Bible reading for the day, he tries to clear his mind, sit quietly, and listen to God. Have you ever tried this?

At first, it is hard to clear your mind. But here is the key: set a stopwatch initially for one minute. Tim did this for a week or two, with no judgment on himself. Pay attention to this point: whether you succeed or fail to clear your mind or hear anything or not, don't judge yourself.

If you practice this consistently, you have better results over time because God honors us when we honor Him. He wants to help us and communicate with us.

After you learn to *be still*, increase the time to two minutes, then three minutes, and so on. Currently, I spend five minutes, though I don't use the stopwatch anymore. Sometimes I hear something from God, but sometimes I can't stop thinking about work and family for the entire five minutes. When I do hear something in my spirit that I believe is from God, I write it down in my journal with the date and label it "Listening Prayer." We don't have to talk or make requests of God when we pray. Listening is also praying.

It's not about the length of time you listen or about *putting God on a stopwatch*. It is about building the discipline of listening prayer. God can talk to you when you are sitting in church, talking to a friend, riding in a car, or going for a walk. You must start somewhere. The stopwatch idea is a tool to build this discipline better. It worked for me.

Sometimes, I go to a park for hours where I do a devotion, prayer, listening prayer, and journaling. I love to spend time with God, which wasn't always the case. As my faith increased through the years, this desire grew. The key is to be still in the presence of God intentionally and listen willingly. As your heart and mind become more receptive, and you practice being still, you have better communication with God. It's the same as when you intentionally practice communicating better with your spouse, friend, or child.

These growth activities are challenging to start and maintain without a mentor, church group, or discipleship program to guide you. Let me be clear: I believe that God can do anything, with anyone, by Himself, anytime. However, I know we are meant to be in a community to love and help each other. I am not sure if the listening prayer with a stopwatch would have worked as well, had I not been through a discipleship program before that.

There are several prayer resources at the end of this book to help you get started.

RECEIVE THROUGH READING THE BIBLE

Another part of our relationship with God and listening to Him comes through reading the Bible. There are more resources than ever before to make this as easy as possible. Many apps have different Bible versions and easy to follow devotional plans, from short to long, including topic-based. Some churches do sermon series on particular books or chapters of the Bible. There are study books available based on specific books of the Bible.

The point is that access to the Bible is easy. Consistently engaging with God's Word is a vital part of building our relationship with Him and listening to Him.

You may be wondering, "How do I receive from God through reading the Bible?"

God communicates with His people through the Bible, similarly to the way you communicate with someone through written letters. Your experience with this is your own. God will reach you in the way He wants to and in the way you are willing to be reached. When I spend repeated days on the same Scripture passage, God reveals different things to me about how to live or a specific concept God is teaching me.

For instance, I read Romans chapter 8 several times on consecutive days. I studied and thought about the following passage:

> So you have not received a spirit that makes you fearful slaves. Instead, you received God's Spirit when he adopted you as his own children. Now we call him, "Abba Father."
>
> (Romans 8:15 NLT)

I thought about the term *adoption*. I reflected on my friends who had adopted children and how they love their adopted children as much as their biological children. Their adopted children have the same rights, responsibilities, and love in their homes as their biological children.

Then I shifted to myself. I am adopted by God the Father. He loves me the same as Jesus, His Son, and gives me equal rights and responsibilities to any of His other children. What an amazing discovery and revelation! As I received this deep into my heart and mind, it became part of my identity and the fabric of my relationship with God. That would never have happened without a regular habit of reading and studying the Bible, along with a willingness to learn and listen through that activity.

When I study and read the Bible, I learn from God, listen to God, and *receive* from God.

BIBLICAL EXAMPLE OF RECEIVE—A HEALED WOMAN

*Just then a woman who had suffered for twelve years with
constant bleeding came up behind him. She touched the fringe
of his robe, for she thought, "If I can just touch his robe, I will
be healed." Jesus turned around, and when he saw her he said,
"Daughter, be encouraged! Your faith has made you well." And
the woman was healed at that moment.*

(Matthew 9:20-22 NLT)

This story is about *believing* and *receiving*. As it relates to
receiving, the simple lesson is this woman (a) came *to* Jesus,
and (b) *expected* to receive from Him. We need to approach
God with the expectation He can and will act.

WHY DOES GOD WANT A RELATIONSHIP WITH ME?

In a word—*love*.

If God has everything, why does He need us? I wondered this,
as well.

Brother Larry Reese, to whom I dedicated this book, teaches
a discipleship class at our church. Brother Larry is a gifted
pastor, teacher, and dear friend.

One day, I gave Brother Larry a ride to the airport. As we
always did, we enjoyed a thought-provoking discussion. But
on this day, God taught me some lessons through Brother
Larry I will never forget.

I asked, "Why does God want an intimate relationship with
us if He doesn't need us?" ("After all," I thought, "God is

all-knowing and all-powerful and can choose to do whatever He wants.") Brother Larry told me it's not because God *needs* us. He *wants* us, which is much better.

Then, he asked this question, "Brian, why do you want to be close to your children?"

I replied, "Because I love them."

Immediately, a light bulb lit up in my head. I had been searching for answers to many questions—"Why should we pray? Why does God want a relationship with me? Why do I need to trust God?" The answer was simple. *It's about love.*

On my way home after dropping off Brother Larry, I couldn't stop thinking about God's love for me. God's love was the answer to so many of my questions. I took a break from my drive and found a park bench. As God taught me, I wrote the following poem.

IT'S ABOUT LOVE

by Brian Goslee

God has a plan for my life because He loves me.

God lets me suffer and grow because He loves me.

God encourages me because He loves me.

God speaks to me through others, the Bible, songs, and directly because He loves me.

God wants to spend time with me because He loves me.

God lets me experience discipline because He loves me.

God gave me the freedom to choose because He loves me.

God wants me to be aligned with His Spirit because He loves me.

God allowed His Son to be crucified on a cross because He loves me.

God wants the best for me because He loves me.

> *So now faith, hope, and love abide, these three; but the greatest of these is love.*
>
> (1 Corinthians 13:13 ESV)

BE IN THE RIGHT POSTURE TO RECEIVE

Accept. Surrender. Yield. Release.

While working on the second stage of this action plan, I considered all these words as titles for this chapter.

Eventually, I chose the word *receive* to summarize these actions. If we truly *receive* Jesus, as described below from the Gospel of John, it permeates every aspect of our lives. It results in *accepting, surrendering*, and *yielding* to His way of living, instead of ours. It results in *releasing* those things we grip so tightly they get in our way of loving God more than anything else in our lives.

Receiving is a process that requires time and patience. Its many facets contribute to the development of our faith and relationship with God. *Receiving* involves significantly humbling oneself, healing, learning, and growing. This stage can often be long and complex. However, this stage develops the most deep-rooted and long-lasting strength, core, and dependence on God. It is worth it!

As with all the stages of the plan, receiving God and yielding to Him are ongoing processes for the rest of our lives. Seek out a mentor, coach, or small group to help you in this process at your local church or ctfaith.com.

OPEN HAND-OPEN HEART

Did you ever notice that if you want to catch a ball, it works better when your hands are open? Remember our illustration in Chapter 2? I asked you to picture yourself with your left hand open, receiving a gift. For many, a baseball glove fits on our left hand. If we have good posture, with our glove open, we increase the chance of catching the ball. If your hand, or baseball mitt, is closed, it's not in a position to receive.

It's the same with our hearts and minds. Like a baseball glove, our hearts must be open and facing God. To receive from God, you need an *open hand, open heart* approach.

One person who learned to believe in God, receive from God, and live with an open hand, open heart posture is my good friend, Tom.

CASE STUDY IN RECEIVING — TOM
A Life Changed Through Faith

> "I went from learning about God
> to pursuing God." - Tom

A great family man and an excellent, loyal manager for a large company, Tom has attended church for many years. He bought into the myth that providing for his family, being a good guy, and accumulating nice things would lead to ultimate fulfillment in life. Many people who believe in God and attend church regularly do not experience the purposeful and fulfilling life God intends for them.

Here are Tom's story and transformation in his words. Take note of the different environments and ways in which he received from God and lived a life of active faith.

> I've been married thirty-four years. We have one grown son who is twenty-seven and on his own.
>
> I would say living a life changed through faith, that part of my journey, started about six years ago when I began attending a new Bible-based church here in town. Before that, we went to church on Sunday, but we went to church, we never really went to God. Since going to this other Bible-based church, we really started to go to God. That was the beginning of the Lord softening my heart. Each service we went to got me a little bit closer to Him.

Then, it's funny how the Lord works. There was a gentleman down the street from where I live; my neighbor, Dick, who I'd played poker with half a dozen times. He reached out to me three different times, "Tom we have a book club, but it's a Jesus-based book club, and we're going to study different books about God and so forth." The first time I said, "No, that's not really me." The second time, I said again, "You know, it's not really me," but in my heart, I knew what the answer was. The third time—and I thank him to this day for asking and pursuing me three times—I said, "Yes."

I was very nervous coming in, but what I quickly learned was it was a half dozen normal guys just all seeking God. The first book we studied together was *Beautiful Outlaw* by John Eldredge. It talks about the fact that Jesus was not just this prim and proper guy. He was a guy you could get to know. That was the beginning of my heart starting to soften by being there with a bunch of guys. When you go to a big church like I do, they tell you that you need a small group or some other mechanism outside of church if you really want to lean in and learn about God. And that's what Dick's basement book club was all about.

In one of the last chapters of the second book we did by John Eldredge, the question was, "What is your next step in the journey?" I prayed about that question a lot. I knew that

Thursday night when we all got together, my next step was to take discipleship class.

This discipleship class is a one-year journey. You go once a week with homework and assignments that are very involved and require much prayer and reflection.

That experience moved me from learning about God to pursuing God.

It was about that time that I bought an entire Bible CD set and listened to the whole Bible from start to finish while driving to work. I moved from listening about God to actually pursuing God.

Now I feel God more. I know He's there, and I've never in my life felt that until about the last year. It's an absolutely amazing feeling. Open the door, and He's there; just ask.

My view for the past thirty years was to work hard, make money, get a nice car, be successful, and take care of your family. All those things are good, but they leave you hollow. You can get that new car, and you're happy for a month. Then you realize, "Okay, what's next?" It never fills you up; it just never fills you up.

I sold my newer car and bought an old truck. People looked at me like, "Tom, what's wrong with you? You know you've changed." And I tell them, "You know, I'm okay." I made the same amount of money, but I took that money I saved on the car payment and gave it all to the church. I did it because I wanted to do it. I wasn't pressured to do it.

That is definitely not where I was a few years ago. I held onto my money. My heart was driven toward taking care of my family, making sure we had nice things. I was pursuing all that most of my life.

Finally, I started to realize, "Okay, that's nice, but not important." I wish I would have learned that at twenty-five, and not forty-five. I think it's harder when you're raising a family, and you're in that provider mode. When you're in that provider mode, it becomes the number one priority thing. And I let that become the number one priority.

There were a couple of times in my life when the Lord tried to shake me. I was driving home from work one day, my rear axle broke, and I hit an embankment. As the car started to roll over, I leaned over to the right. When I say I leaned over, something pushed me over. I felt it, I absolutely felt it. Miraculously, I got up and walked away. The ambulance guy said that as he was pulling down the hill and he saw the car with the roof crashed in, he said, "This will be a one- or two-bagger." That's what they thought. They immediately thought, "Whoever's in there is dead." And I walked away from that.

I knew it was a wakeup call. I started to listen, but I didn't pursue God the way I do now. I learned about God, but I didn't really pursue Him. I would say God pursued me, but because I was in such a provider mode for my family, I didn't allow Him to be a priority.

I don't know if my journey has been similar to others because I wouldn't say that I had this great thing that happened, walked up on the stage, and I was immediately saved. For me, it was a multi-year journey of God softening my heart, then moving from learning about God to pursuing God, and now looking at Him as a friend. God has been that friend. Jesus has been that friend, and He's helped me in so many ways. It's been an amazing journey so far.

THE DESIRES OF YOUR HEART

In Tom's story, we see he experienced growth through many pathways: church, small group, discipleship school, and so on. Through activating his faith, God changed his heart. Tom used to pursue money and things; now he seeks God and the things God wants him to pursue.

Dick's heart faced God when he obeyed God by inviting his neighbor multiple times to his basement book group. Both men demonstrated changed lives on the outside because of the transformation of their hearts on the inside.

* * *

Recently, I read a passage in Psalm 37 that I have read many times before. This time, though, I received it differently.

> *Delight yourself in the Lord, and he will give you the desires of your heart.*
>
> *(Psalm 37:4 ESV)*

In the past, I thought this meant "Believe in God. Do more good stuff than bad stuff, and God will give you what you want, for the most part." I know, quite the unscholarly interpretation, not to mention inaccurate!

But this time, I realized God gives me the desires of my heart *twice*. First, He *replaces* my desires with His as I receive them. Second, once I align the desires of my heart with His (as much as possible in our human conditions), God *gifts* them to me. So, He replaces the desires of my heart, then gifts them to me.

God did this in my life. Over time, my desires started to match up with His vision for my life. He sent people and plans into my life that advanced the calling and destiny He had for me. I see this clearly because He planted these desires and made them happen. Understand, however, this is not typically a quick process! We need to put our fast food and microwave mindset aside while we patiently wait on God.

ACCEPT

To receive something fully, we need to accept it. Have you ever had a hard time accepting something? Maybe it was a situation or a stance someone took that didn't sit well with you.

Several years ago, I read a Bible passage in the Gospel of Matthew that really caught me off guard. Jesus said to His disciples, "*I have not come to bring peace, but a sword.*" I read it several times to make sure I read it right. I thought Jesus would say the opposite. After all, He's the Prince of Peace. Why would He say this?

To answer, consider the vital point Jesus made. He came so everyone would *choose* to repent, accept Him, follow Him, and have a relationship with God through Him.

Jesus needed to draw the line with His followers. They had to decide, just like we do—either Jesus is the leader of our lives, or He is not. Have you ever had to tell someone, "That is where I draw the line!"? Well, Jesus drew the line.

According to the Gospel of Matthew, Jesus said,

> *So everyone who acknowledges me before men, I also will acknowledge before my Father who is in heaven, but whoever denies me before men, I also will deny before my Father who is in heaven. Do not think that I have come to bring peace to the earth. I have not come to bring peace, but a sword. For I have come to set a man against his father, and a daughter against her mother, and a daughter-in-law against her mother-in-law. And a person's enemies will be those of his own household. Whoever loves father or mother more than me is not worthy of me, and whoever loves son or daughter more than me is not worthy of me. And whoever does not take his cross and follow me is not worthy of me. Whoever finds his life will lose it, and whoever loses his life for my sake will find it. "Whoever receives you receives me, and whoever receives me receives him who sent me."*

> *(Matthew 10:32-40 ESV)*

Jesus is clear: Either you're with Him, or you're against Him.

This passage is sobering, especially the part about family turning against one another. It's not that Jesus wants a father to be against his son or a mother against her daughter. Following Jesus doesn't have to mean you are enemies with those in your household. It means there's no messing around. There will be people who choose God and face rejection from their families.

People have to choose sides. And your choice is more important than anything else. You either accept and believe Jesus is your Savior, or you don't. Either you accept and believe in Father, Son, and Holy Spirit, or you don't. Like any good parent, God holds us accountable.

If you accept and believe, you start down an incredible life journey of discovery and purpose. Your life is changed through faith as you go through the development stages.

If you do not accept and believe in God or Jesus as your Savior at this time, I invite you to continue reading and investigating. You matter to God. He loves you and is waiting for you! God has a plan of blessing and fulfillment for you when He is the Lord of your life.

To *receive it*, we commit to God's way of doing life over the way our culture tells us to do life. We submit to God and His Word, instead of materialism and me-ism.

THE DAY I ACCEPTED JESUS

I remember the day I accepted Jesus as my Savior. Although I had been to church in my youth, it was not until I was 33 that I made this important decision. I attended a Christian businessmen's luncheon for several months. On this day, while talking to some of the leaders after lunch, one of them asked, "Brian, have you accepted Jesus as your Savior?"

I answered, "I'm not sure."

He said, "Well, let's make sure."

We sat down, and several men prayed with me. I admitted my sin, need for a Savior, and acceptance of Jesus as the Lord of my life. It was very powerful. Eleven years later, I was baptized.

SURRENDER AND YIELD

Belief in God and acceptance of Jesus Christ as our Savior are huge steps. However, if this is all we do to activate our faith, we won't get far. To experience all that God has planned for us, we need to advance down the road of our spiritual journey.

We need to come to the difficult, but life-defining, conclusion that *His way is always better than our way*. Not easier—*better*. More importantly, we surrender our life to Him and yield to His plans for us. To make room for God's way, we remove some other things.

> We need to come to the difficult, but life-defining, conclusion that *His way is always better than our way.*

My good friend, Trevor, demonstrates the concepts of surrendering and yielding to God. But it wasn't always that way.

TREVOR SANTOR—AUTHOR, COACH, PASTOR, FRIEND

Trevor Santor is a baseball coach, author, and personal friend. He is a Pastor of Discipleship and Athletics at a church and the founder and CEO of Baseball Genesis. Before that, he coached high school and college baseball, mentored players, and invited them to activities at his church.

Due to multiple injuries and coaching changes, Trevor's baseball career experienced setbacks throughout high school and early college. He followed his dream to play baseball professionally and focused on himself and the game he loved. Halfway through college, Trevor transferred to a new school because He felt God called him there. As the fall exhibition season began, he arrived at this new school with high expectations and excitement.

In the first game with his new team, Trevor hit a wall. Literally. He ran face-first into a brick wall in center field while chasing down a fly ball. With blood running down his face and his knee, he lay there, while students and players rushed out to attend to him and pray with him.

In those moments, God told him, "Trevor, everything will be okay. Just place your trust in Me. Place your trust in Me, Trevor." He felt the peace and love of Jesus like he never had before, lying injured on a baseball warning track. Trevor surrendered fully to Jesus right then and there. He was ready and willing to *receive* from God.

Over the next several months, as he recovered from a fractured face and patella, God worked in his heart and sent friends to minister to him. When Trevor returned to the field six months later, he played for the Lord instead of himself. He went on to finish a strong collegiate career, athletically and academically, eventually earning an MBA.

After college, Trevor coached baseball, founded a ministry, and wrote a book called *Baseball Genesis: Living for Christ Through the Game of Baseball.* Trevor runs a faith-based baseball training center called Baseball Genesis where he trains baseball players spiritually, mentally, and physically through the game they love. He also serves on staff at his church as Pastor of Discipleship and Athletics. Trevor's mission is to grow God's Kingdom through the game of baseball. Trevor received and yielded to God fully in his life!

And, yes. Trevor made the catch!

RELEASE

Receiving from God involves releasing those things we grip tightly. Often, they get in our way of loving God more than anything else in our lives. In the Gospels, Jesus taught His disciples to release their lives to Him and accept His way.

> *"If you cling to your life, you will lose it; but if you give up your life for me, you will find it."*
>
> (Matthew 10:39 NLT)

So what do we need to release? We need to release *our controlling grip* on

- What we want
- When we want it
- How we get it

It doesn't make much sense to us initially, but when we release control to God, we gain freedom.

Why?

Chasing pleasure enslaves us because it never satisfies. To fill the void, we continue the chase and try to control our lives without God and become trapped. When we submit to God's ways, we stop the cycle of seeking satisfaction in temporary pleasures. We are free.

Our pursuit of peace, prestige, and accomplishment, outside of God's will for us, never ends in fulfillment. When we release control to God and pursue what is true, honorable, and in His will for us, we escape the bondage of the world's ways and experience freedom in Christ.

> Our pursuit of peace, prestige, and accomplishment, outside of God's will for us, never ends in fulfillment.

God waits for us with open arms of unconditional love and acceptance. He desires to exchange our problems, struggles, and desires for the abundant life He promises. God waits patiently with an open and welcoming posture.

UNCLENCH THOSE HANDS

Not long ago, I talked with someone who held on tightly to a bad habit. This person had every defense for why there was nothing wrong with it or as bad as some other things people did. I prayed for God to give me something to say to help this person. I'm not sure if what I said made a difference, but this is what I said:

You are holding on so tightly to this sin area—gripping it so tightly—that until you let it go, and give it to God, you will not be able to receive what He has for you.

As I said it, I illustrated by holding my hand out in a fist and then opening it slowly.

Accepting God and receiving Him is that simple. It may not be easy to do, but it is a simple concept. Yield to His way instead of yours! You will be more at peace if you remember it's not about what you want, but rather what God wants for you.

We need to unclench our hands, let go of greed, and be less consumed with material things. Perhaps you put too much time and energy into a hobby or even an area of habitual sin. Maybe you have something *good* blocking your approach to God, like climbing higher in your career or coaching all of your kids' sports teams. These are not bad by themselves. *The problem occurs when anything takes the number one spot over your relationship with God.*

Even good things can get in the way of what God wants to do through your life. Here are some examples of good things that can potentially become idols and ultimately drive your motivations in life, instead of God:

- Trying to be the perfect parent
- Advancing your career
- Volunteering at an unhealthy level
- Idolizing your kids' accomplishments

These things can get in the way of your relationship with God if they are the answer to the question "What drives you?"

For me, the answer to "What drives you?" was to be a great dad and provide for my family. I thought as long as I did that, I was entitled to sinful activities once in a while (which meant every day). I thought, "I'm not hurting anyone. I need to relax from this tough job of being the best dad and family man that I can be." Wow, how noble and humble I was!

If you loosen your grip on chasing these things and open your hands to receive God, you will find your life. It will take time, but the most rewarding things require time, effort, and personal investment.

What should drive us is a one-word answer: **God.** Our relationship with Him is paramount in our lives. To fully *receive* God and all He plans for us, we need to *make room*. We need to release our sin areas, idols, and control of our lives to God. When we do, it makes room for healing to occur.

HEALING

When we pursue God and spend time developing a relationship with Him, we receive and experience healing. Why is that so important?

Let's think about it in physical terms. Have you ever had a wound or cut that would not close or heal by itself? You needed care, perhaps stitches, bandaging, and treatment to properly heal. At about twelve years old, I needed stitches after making a peanut butter and jelly sandwich. While reaching into the cupboard for the peanut butter, I cut my forearm on a large knife facing point-up in the sink's dish drainer, which was below the cabinet. To this day, *all* knives go face-down in the dishwasher and dish drainer at the Goslee's house. Lesson learned!

When it comes to growing our faith and recovering from our wounds, God is the source of our healing. He heals our wounds and provides care. Yes, we may receive medical care, mental health care, addiction recovery care, and more, but, if we let Him, God is with us and the core of our healing.

JULIE — FRIEND, SINGER, MINISTRY LEADER, VICTOR

"I saw the dove and it took my breath away."
-Julie

Julie is an amazing servant of God, an incredible worship singer, and a great caretaker of God's people. She is a tremendous leader of a large and vibrant Celebrate Recovery program. Julie experienced great pain through most of her life, as the result of a difficult upbringing, abusive relationships, addiction, and more. As she shared her story with me, three things stuck out:

1. She survived and thrived in her relationship with God and others despite the sheer amount of pain she experienced.

2. God uses *every* aspect and depth of her past pain to help Julie minister to others in an effective and loving way.

3. God is with Julie, saved her, healed her, and used her struggles to bring glory to Him and accomplish His plans.

None of these could have occurred without healing. Julie had to receive God's healing to experience a life changed through faith in Him. Although God planted the seed when Julie was ten years old, it did not mature until nearly thirty years later.

Julie's full story is available at ctfaith.com, but here are two key elements from her account. First, at ten-years-old, Julie received an invitation from a friend to know God. Invitations to and from friends are avenues God uses to help people receive from Him. After planting the seed of faith, Julie knew God was there, even during the next thirty years of extreme struggles.

Second, Julie reached out for and received the healing from God she desperately needed to recover from her past painful life. It started when she reached out, became sober, and continued into deep spiritual healing. Both aspects of Julie's story are shared below in her words.

EXPERIENCING JESUS AT A YOUNG AGE

My life's been dramatically changed through faith. I guess there were several series of events that brought me to faith and then also changed it over the years. My life has been, or at least was, pretty hectic and crazy, especially as a younger person. There was one constant, and that was my knowledge there was a power greater than myself out there.

I wasn't raised in a Christian home. I don't think my parents ever told me about Jesus or anything like that. But, luckily for me, the Lord pursued me even at a young age. I knew people went to church and did things, but since it wasn't my experience in my home life, I was always intrigued by that. So, anytime I had an opportunity to go to a church with someone, I would go. But my first experience with Jesus, gratefully for me, was when I was about ten years old.

My first encounter was on the bathroom floor in a girlfriend's trailer. We lived out in the country when I was a kid, on kind-of a farm my dad put together for us. My friend's name was Tina. I'll never forget it. I've never been around her as an adult. I don't remember a lot of things from my youth, but I do remember this occasion. We went to some church event, and I was asking questions. We were hiding like little girls do, and sitting on the floor talking. She had her Bible. I think that was probably the first time I'd ever experienced a Bible. Like kids do, not always with completely accurate information, she said, "If you want to know who Jesus is, you should read this part of this book," and she turned to Revelation. I'd never even seen a Bible before. I tried to read some of it, but it looked scary and crazy, as it would to somebody who didn't know what that was about.

However, what I know to be true, was that I experienced something that day. I said, "I don't really understand this," but as you see how my child life was, you'll understand I had a real "missing" of something in my heart. I didn't trust or have somebody that I felt really safe with. And I thought if this was that person, then I needed that person. So, on that floor, sitting by the bathtub in that girl's bathroom that day, I just said, "Jesus, I want you to be my guy."

I definitely had a true, real experience. I still remember it vividly today, at almost fifty-two years old. That's when I found out Jesus was real. Now that's a little different than necessarily having a relationship with him, but I knew in that moment that He was real, He existed, and He could be that guy for me. So that was the start of my knowledge of Him, but not [necessarily] my relationship with Him.

FROM SOBRIETY, TO DREAMING, TO SINGING, TO HEALING

I got to the point where I was sick and tired of drinking. I felt like I couldn't imagine my life drinking anymore, and I could not imagine my life not drinking.

I remember sitting in the parking lot of that church, drinking, sitting outside of it, just crying and drinking beer looking at the church and saying, "I'm going to need you to do something because I can't do it. I need you to help me. I'm begging you. I'm sitting here in the parking lot of this building that you're supposed to be in, and I need you to do something for me."

Shortly after that, I got what I believe to be a few different little intervention signs from the Lord. I went to an AA meeting at a church right by where I lived. The day I walked in, there was a big dove on the wall. I saw the dove, and it took my breath away. I was like, "the Holy Spirit's here." I stopped drinking that day and I never drank again. It's been almost sixteen years since I drank. That night, that was it. I knew I was done.

When I walked in that room, I felt God say, "It's time. It's time. You begged. You've been through this." It's almost like I look back now and He said, "Okay, I've spared you to a degree. You went through all this, but now I've got something for you to do. You're welcome. Now it's time for you to do this for Me." And I said, "Okay." So, I started working the program, jumped in with both feet, and never looked back.

I went to AA for about three years. This is the great part about God. I was going to church and getting into the children's ministry, and the Lord told me, "I want you to start singing again." And I was like, "Yeah, I don't know, Lord, if I can." He said, "No, but it's going to be different. You're singing for me this time." I thought, "Oh, I'm going to be singing Jesus music or something." So I started. That was the first time I heard contemporary Christian music. I was about 40 years old.

My kids were getting into their teenage years. We decided we wanted to check out some other churches that were a little bit more contemporary. I had about three years of recovery under my belt, so I was feeling pretty good.

One Sunday morning, while driving to a new church we were checking out, I said to my kids, "I had the weirdest dream last night." They're like, "Mom, [not] another dream!"

I said, "But listen. It was weird. I was in this building—a church or a school, but I'm not sure which. I didn't understand why I was there. There was this real tall guy, and I was hanging on his leg while he's dragging me. I said, "I need you to teach me about Jesus." In the dream, I said, "I don't know if I'm in a church or a school. It doesn't matter, but I need you to be my teacher."

So, we go into the church and sit down. The announcement guy comes up and the first thing he says, "Hey guys, guess what? We're going to be planting a church at the local high school." My kids looked at me and said, "A church in a school." Their ears [perked up] like little doggy ears. And then the man said, "There's a meeting today. If you're interested, you should come." I looked at my kids and said, "I guess we're going to a meeting today." And they're all like, "yeah." So, that day after the service, we walked into this room. [The pastor of the new church plant was there]. I walked in, and my middle son Fran said, "Well, there's your tall guy." And I'm thinking, "I guess here we are." I never questioned if that was where I should be. I just moved forward with that church plant, and things just happened.

[One of the first things that happened was meeting a member of the planting team]. He said, "Do you sing?" I said, "Yeah." He asked me to be on the team. I never met the guy before. He'd never heard me sing.

It was God saying, "Here's exactly what I want you to do. Now, are you going to choose to be obedient and do it?" So, I started doing those things. I was thinking, "So this guy [the pastor] is going to teach me about You [God], then I'm going to understand, right?"

That's where I learned about my Father [God] and how to process God as the Father. As I started listening to Pastor Paul teach, he explained the Bible in a way I could actually understand and relate to it.

I knew Jesus. Jesus was my bud. He was my relationship. He was my everything. The Holy Spirit, I could communicate with Him and he could give me peace. Now, I [also] had this Godly Father that Pastor Paul talked about. God the Father helped me to forgive my father for everything and anything he may or may not have done. When we're kids, we think one thing—we don't know. As you become a parent, you see things differently. Then I saw God as a father, and I felt like I finally had this whole picture—this unified picture.

That's where my journey of healing really started. I was sober for a few years. I was able to start growing and start seeing what it meant to be a fully engaged follower of Christ. What did it mean for me? For me, it meant healing. It's not about doing; it was about my healing because I can't do for anybody else until I can feel okay about myself. When we started Celebrate Recovery, it was the perfect combination for me: a Christ-centered recovery program. It's working a program of recovery and getting in fellowship.

Now I have this whole community of people who are willing to talk about the same things I've discussed.

This is how my life was. This is what happened. Here's what God did, and here's what I do today.

I'm not ashamed of it because God forgave me. He doesn't use shame or guilt to convince me of anything. He convicts me about where I need to go today.

It's not about what happened back then; it's about where I'm going tomorrow. It's completely flip-flopped my life as you can tell.

Yes, I have two marriages behind me. Are there things I wish were different? Yeah, I guess so. But in the same respect, I'll look at it and think there are so many, many people that I can relate to in so many different situations. I've walked through two of my best friends losing children—one to suicide, one to a horrible accident. I'm even able to walk them through that and help them to keep Jesus in that process because the Holy Spirit has just given me some strange anointing to be able to walk through that with people. I've ministered to a lot of families in really difficult situations because God took a long time with a long track record, to fortify my faith in him.

Today, I believe that ten-year-old in the bathroom was given the gift of faith. That's what I believe. I tell people I feel blessed to have been given that gift because I've always known somebody was there. I wasn't always participating in the relationship too well, but he was always there. Always. Always.

WHAT DO WE RECEIVE?

What do we receive through our actions and transformation in the *receive* stage? Deep into our hearts, we receive from God:

- His love
- His mercy
- His grace
- His forgiveness
- His acceptance
- His healing

What an awesome list! I encourage you to not only *believe* in God and who He is, but also to *receive* Him deep into your heart and life. You can do this through *accepting* His truths, *submitting* to His authority, *surrendering* to His ways, *yielding* to His plans for you, and *releasing* all your junk that gets in the way.

You might think, "I want to receive from God. How do I do that?" First, be patient and realize this will happen over time. Second, at the end of this chapter, there are practical steps and tips for this stage. Third, have a mentor or mature Christian come alongside you in this process. This person needs to be someone you can trust and can keep things in confidence. You will share with them where you are in your journey of faith. A pastor, small group through your church, or a discipleship class or similar program is very helpful in this process. For that reason, we have online small groups, courses, and faith development coaching available at ctfaith.com.

Once we *Believe* and *Receive* from God consistently, we live differently. Our faith becomes an active daily faith. We mature in our faith and live for God, not for ourselves. In other words, we start to *Live It*!

⬛ ACTIVATE YOUR FAITH—RECEIVE

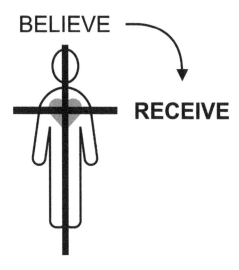

RECEIVE

As we believe in faith, we can begin to *receive* God in our hearts, along with all He offers us. It is one thing to believe, but another to *receive*, which is an integral part of our relationship and faith journey with God. It takes time.

RECEIVE THROUGH PRAYER

Lord, Let Your wisdom take over in place of my thinking.

Let Your Spirit of faith and boldness replace my spirit of fear and insecurity.

Do a work in me that gives me hope in You for who You are, not for blessings.

I pray for faith and peace instead of fear in my finances.

I pray for hope and freedom instead of frustration and bondage.

I pray for Your plans for me to take place in Your timing.

I surrender ALL of this, ALL I have, and ALL I am into Your hands. Amen.

PRAYER TIPS: Try structuring your prayer time as follows:

- Thank God for something specific
- Repent of your sins and ask forgiveness
- Pray for someone else
- Pray for yourself and your family
- Listen for two minutes—quiet your mind and try to hear God in your spirit

RECEIVE THROUGH THE BIBLE

Read the excerpt below at least three days in a row. Each day list the three words or phrases from the passage that speak to you the most and why. (You can repeat listings if that is what happens.) For maximum impact, share this activity with someone and compare notes.

> *Even before he made the world, God loved us and chose us in Christ to be holy and without fault in his eyes. God decided in advance to adopt us into his family by bringing us to himself through Jesus Christ.*
>
> *(Ephesians 1:4-5 NLT)*

Day 1

Today, which word or phrase from the passage spoke to you the most? Why?

Day 2

Which word or phrase from the passage spoke to you the most? Why?

Day 3

Which word or phrase from the passage spoke to you the most? Why?

RECEIVE THROUGH RELATIONSHIPS

Choose one of the following action items to do and share it with a close Christian friend or in your online CTFaith program.

☐ LISTENING PRAYER: Try the Listening Prayer activity pg 53 at least three days in a row this week immediately after reading your Bible devotional. Practice it for two minutes. Write down in your journal anything God puts in your mind or heart.

☐ IT'S ABOUT LOVE: Read the poem *It's About Love* pg 58 again. Are there any statements you don't believe? Write them down and discuss them with your friend, coach, or small group. Find out what they believe. It is not about the correct answer or who is right; it is about engaging in thought and conversation and learning more.

☐ ACCEPTING JESUS: Have you accepted Jesus as the Lord and Savior of your life? If so, what were the circumstances surrounding that decision? If you haven't, what is holding you back? Are you unsure if you have? Talk about your answer(s) with your friend, coach, or small group. You can also reach out to us at ctfaith.com

RECEIVE THROUGH A RENEWED MIND

Unclenching Your Grip

- ☐ Finish this sentence, "On the weekend, I can't wait to _____."

What's the first thing that comes to mind (honestly)? What did you put in the blank?

Perhaps it is healthy and in balance, but maybe it's not. Prayerfully consider if you need to unclench your grip on this area and adjust your life. Often, we need to release something in our lives to make room for time with God.

What do you need to release?

- ☐ I need to release _____ to make room for God.

When you release this, God puts into your hands better things He has for you.

RECEIVE: JOURNAL TIME

Based on your answers above, think about one action you can take, or an adjustment you can make to help you make room for God and receive from Him.

Write down any changes or adjustments you think of:

Do you have an area of hurt, hang-up, pain, or addiction that is hard to break or affecting your progress? If so, reach out for help from your church, a family member, friend, or celebraterecovery.com.

Know that God can crush those areas with His mighty healing power and the power of His Holy Spirit for those who trust in Him and seek true repentance!

Need guidance and encouragement on this journey? Join an online small group, take the Changed Through Faith Action Plan course, or sign up for faith development coaching at ctfaith.com.

CHAPTER 6
LIVE IT

What you have learned and received and heard and seen in me—
practice these things, and the peace of God will be with you.

(Philippians 4:9 ESV)

Even if we *believe* and *receive*, our lives won't change unless we *live out* our identity as Christians. Many of us do a great job living out our faith on Sundays, and maybe once a week at a small group meeting, but when we're at home or in our careers, we often don't do as well.

Once we consistently *believe* and *receive* from God, we naturally want to experience something more. We want to experience fullness of life and His peace that surpasses understanding. We may not verbalize it that way, but most of us reach a point when we ask, "Isn't there more to life than this?"

The answer is a resounding, "Yes!"

Wherever we are in life, God has more for us: more blessings, more peace, more meaning. To experience them, we must boldly follow Him and actively live out our faith.

Living it means living out an active faith in Christ every day. In this chapter, we look at many ways to *live it* in our relationship with God and others.

It takes *active* faith.

ACTIVE FAITH

> *What good is it, dear brothers and sisters, if you say you have faith but don't show it by your actions?*
>
> *(James 2:14 NLT)*

When we *live it*, faith becomes an action verb — ignited action that flows out of our love for God and our love from God.

Active faith means we don't go to church on Sunday and merely try to be a *good person* for the rest of the week. Those are great places to start, but our faith must be a seven-day-a-week faith, not only a Sunday faith. We learn and grow throughout the week by studying the Bible, listening to worship music, praying, and being in intentional Christian relationships. These activities contribute to an active faith in Christ. We also serve, encourage, and love others.

A word of caution, however. It is not simply doing the activities that leads to an active faith; it's doing them with a heart that seeks God and faces Him. It is imperative to have a heart and mind that is receptive to God and eager to learn from Him.

GOD TAUGHT ME HOW TO LIVE IT

Not long after I experienced amazing healing in my life, I flew to Florida to interview for a community college teaching position. During my lifetime in Ohio, I never taught at the college level, so this was an exciting opportunity. I was called for the interview the same day of my healing, November 1, 2013. Naturally, I believed this was "meant to be."

With brand-new joy and freedom in my heart, I was open and aware of God's presence. I had my radar up for any possible prompting to minister to others.

On the plane, I sat next to a woman who seemed disturbed. We made small talk, but it didn't take long for her to share she was returning home to Florida after attending her adult son's funeral, who had recently passed away. She hurt very much. As she shared her story over the next couple of hours, I listened attentively and prayed silently. At the end of the flight, I shared a new Christian song I thought might encourage her. As we departed the plane, she said, "You were not put next to me by accident. God sent you here today as an angel."

My job interview went well, and I had some great time with the Lord. Throughout the entire trip, I was full of joy from the Holy Spirit.

A member of the interview group told me privately to expect a call with the job offer, but it never came. I did not get the position. In my disappointment, I asked God questions like,

"Why would you take me to Florida, have a great interview process, and not give me the job?"

As the months went on, I didn't get many answers. Then one day, I realized God took me on that trip not to get a teaching job, but to learn to pursue *Him*. He wanted to teach me a new way to live *every day*. God showed me I could be praise-filled, joyful, and free and to have my radar up to minister to others at His prompting. He had to take me out of town for a few days, out of my routine, with my newly healed mind, body, and spirit, to teach me a new way to live!

LIVE IT BY PUTTING GOD FIRST

I never thought I would make God truly number one in my life. I knew I was supposed to; I even knew I wanted to, but I believed I couldn't do it. My hierarchy of priorities on most days was (1) family, (2) job, and (3) God. I thought about God as one segment of my life. I did not exchange my desires to pursue His will for me. God, however, taught me a new way to live as I followed Him and lived out my faith more consistently and actively.

Believing in God and putting Him first are keys to experiencing life as the person God has called you to be. It is also the key to eternal life, as Jesus reminded us. If you think that is impossible, it's not. It will take time, but it can happen.

For God so loved the world, that he gave his only Son, that whoever believes in him should not perish but have eternal life.

(John 3:16 ESV)

LIVE IT BY FACING YOUR HEART TOWARD GOD

Throughout both the Old and New Testament, a central theme is, "Seek the Lord your God with all of your heart."

> *But from there you will seek the Lord your God and you will find him, if you search after him with all your heart and with all your soul.*
>
> *(Deuteronomy 4:29 ESV)*

> *Trust in the Lord with all your heart, and do not lean on your own understanding.*
>
> *(Proverbs 3:5 ESV)*

> *You will seek me and find me, when you seek me with all your heart.*
>
> *(Jeremiah 29:13 ESV)*

> *And you shall love the Lord your God with all your heart and with all your soul and with all your mind and with all your strength.*
>
> *(Mark 12:30 ESV)*

God cares about our behavior, but ultimately, He cares about the condition of our heart and which way it is facing. Is our heart open and facing Him, or closed to Him and looking to the world?

In the verses above, God reminds us to face our hearts toward Him, full of love for Him, giving it everything we have—heart, soul, mind, and strength!

LIVE IT BY PURSUING GOD

With our hearts open and facing God, we pursue Him daily. Think about how you spend your time each day. What do you chase? Where do you focus the majority of your time, talent, and money? We must pursue God more strongly than we seek everything else.

God always pays attention to us. We run after Him because He is awesome and loving. When you build a great relationship, you desire to spend time with that person, to learn about them, and to listen to them. We need to pursue God, pray to Him, and listen to Him intentionally.

PURSUE

by Brian Goslee

Pursue God's truths, not culture's lies

Pursue Jesus, not your own agenda

Pursue the fruits of the Spirit, not the works of the flesh

Pursue the things above, not the things on earth

Pursue Godly riches, not earthly riches

Pursue eternal life, not temporal happiness

Pursue righteousness, not being right

Pursue joy, not happiness

Pursue your calling, not your job

Pursue truth, not what you want to hear

Pursue God's promises, not the comfort of good enough

LIVE IT BY SEEKING GOD THROUGH HIS WORD

The *Pursue* poem talks about pursuing God's truths and promises. One of the best ways you can do this is through the Bible. Throughout this book, I share key Scripture verses. I would not live a life of active faith without pursuing God through the Bible.

The Bible is God's Word for all of us. We experience it personally and at our own pace through following a consistent Bible reading plan that works for you. Don't worry about how big or small your goals are, and don't compare your Bible accomplishments to others. Remember, your journey is unique.

Today, there are more ways to interact with the Bible than ever before. There are mobile apps for Bible reading with tracks arranged by topics such as the Changed Through Faith and YouVersion Bible apps. Some people like listening; others prefer reading. Some people use a hard copy; others an electronic device. There are one or two year plans to read the Bible.

I like to write and highlight in my hard copy Bible, alternating with an electronic app for highlighting and notetaking. Some people study with others in a group; some choose an individual approach. There are many different translations of the Bible. I frequently read and research in the English Standard Version (ESV), New International Version (NIV), and New Living Translation (NLT) versions. In the Activate Your Faith sections of this book, review the Bible activities and resources designed to help you.

One of my friends listened to the Bible on his daily commute to work every day, which changed his relationship with God into one of active faith. I read individual books of the Bible as

God leads me to them through prayer, sermons, or interactions with other people. My preference is to read larger chunks of the Bible, but not every single day. My wife reads smaller portions every day following a disciplined plan. Each way works.

Regardless of how you do it, reading and receiving God's Word through the Bible grows your faith and relationship with Him. God reveals wisdom, knowledge, plans, and love in and through the Bible.

Other ways to learn from God's Word: listen to sermons live at church or online, and read Christian books. However, be sure you don't substitute these for learning directly from God in prayer, worship, and personal Bible study.

GORDON WICKERT—AUTHOR, HUSBAND, FATHER, FRIEND

My friend, Gordon Wickert, pursues God to the fullest every day by helping others see the H.O.P.E of God's Word in a creative way.

To some people, Gordon seems like a regular guy. He works for a large company, attends church, serves faithfully, and has a great relationship with his wife and four children. However, Gordon is not a regular guy, because he loves Jesus and follows Him with extraordinary boldness and passion—he lives it!

Gordon founded a wonderful ministry called *H.O.P.E. In Numbers*. (Holding Onto God's Promises Everywhere). God gifted him with a phenomenal talent to see Scripture and hope in the numbers all around him. Every day during break time at his job, he walks the parking lot and makes short videos, teaching people how to see God's Word and Bible verses in the numbers around us every day: on cars, on signs, on receipts, you name it. Gordon teaches people how to do this as a guest speaker at events and shares it in his everyday activities like shopping. He wrote a great book called *Hope In Numbers* to share his gift and teach the world how to do it as well.

I apply Gordon's ministry concepts every day. I relate numbers around me to Scripture verses and talk to others about it. I memorize Bible verses, so I always have them with me. Through these practices, I reprogram the messages that flow through my mind every day. Gordon's methodology helps me live out my faith by frequently seeking God through the Bible.

LIVE IT BY BEING FAITHFUL THROUGH PAIN

When we live out an active faith in Christ, we discover we are in a fight. God has something great for you that may be hard to see. The enemy has something terrible for you that he makes easy to see. The enemy, called Satan, will tempt you and try to distract you from living out an active faith in Christ.

Jesus offers us more!

> *The thief comes only to steal and kill and destroy. I came that they may have life and have it abundantly.*
>
> *(John 10:10 ESV)*

Realize we are in a fight. There will be pain along the way, but God's blessing follows the pain.

The enemy wants to derail you from living the life God has for you. One of the tools the enemy will use is pain: in relationships, in situations, and even physical pain. Not all physical pain is from Satan, but he will use all types of pain, and especially how we think about the pain, to distract us.

Our choices or other circumstances may cause pain. It can be brought on by running or hiding from God. Pain can result from exhaustion, which makes us vulnerable to the enemy's attacks.

> God can use the pain in our lives to strengthen us for the battle that lies ahead.

God forges our character to be more like His and can use pain to grow us. Jesus experienced pain—lots of it. We need to identify which pain God uses to make us into His image and which is meant to derail us by the enemy. As He did for Jesus, God can use the pain in our lives to strengthen us for the battle that lies ahead.

When the pain comes, we need to embrace it and learn from it. If we don't run from it, we identify the lessons God wants to teach us. And when we learn the lessons and pass the test, God's blessing follows the pain.

Turn to the Lord, and He will overcome. That's how we *live it*; we turn to Him with our problems and pain, knowing He is with us, cares about us, and understands. He's forging us into a new creation in Christ. He wants us to learn lessons and pass tests, so we are strengthened and prepared to follow His ways.

CASE STUDY IN LIVING IT—LAUREN

A Life Changed Through Faith

As my daughter entered her teenage years, she struggled with pain in her foot that wouldn't go away. After visits to several specialists, they determined she needed surgery. There wasn't a solid explanation for the pain, as her circumstance was unusual. She underwent surgery, but, unfortunately, the pain returned after a few months.

As with most kids, Lauren enjoyed being active. By the third year with this pain, she became frustrated and challenged by it when walking or engaging in any sport. Her pain was physical, but it also affected her emotionally and spiritually. She loved God and actively lived her faith. It was hard for her to understand how God could allow her to experience this for so long. Have you ever been in that position?

After much prayer and family consultation with doctors, we scheduled another surgery. Over several months, we prayed the doctor would see something different this time and would find the actual cause of her pain. Also, every time my wife prayed, she saw a vision of a spot on Lauren's foot. It represented the injured area and was surrounded by red, indicating pain.

The day of the second operation arrived. While Lauren was in surgery, we sat in the waiting room and prayed.

When the surgery was over, we met the doctor in the post-operative conference room. He believed they took care of the pain for good. What great news!

When the operation began, he said he noticed an area previously hidden during the first surgery. He described it as if someone "removed the ceiling on this room, and you could see right down into it." He believed it revealed the cause of her pain, which he was able to surgically repair. God miraculously answered our specific prayer to let the doctor see something he didn't see before.

While Lauren was in the recovery room, my wife and I went to the hospital cafeteria, where my wife told me an amazing story of God's goodness. When she prayed during Lauren's surgery, she saw the same vision as before, but this time, the whole area was covered in *white*, representing God's healing.

We both broke down in tears over God's goodness. We thanked God in faith and complete gratitude for the vision and for miraculously working through the doctor. We claimed this healing for our daughter. Indeed, the blessing was following the pain.

But, the enemy wasn't finished.

Remember, the enemy uses all types of pain, and how we view the pain, to distract us. As my daughter recovered from surgery, things went well for a while. But, after a month or two, the pain returned.

I'll admit; I started to doubt. Did we get this wrong? Did we make it up? I thought God said He took care of it. Is the pain back for good? Were the vision and the miracle through the doctor not supposed to last?

God encouraged me to take a stand and challenged us to be active in our faith. One night, I went into my daughter's room to talk and pray with her. I had faith, but I also had doubt. I chose faith over fear. I decided to *believe* God over the enemy and taught my daughter to do the same thing.

"Lauren, I am going to tell you something. And even as I am telling you, the enemy is whispering to me not to say it. He's saying I'll look like a fool if I'm wrong, but I am *not wrong* because God is *not wrong*. God wants you to know that He absolutely healed you through that surgery. Don't doubt it. Everything we told you about this time is true. This surgery will take care of your pain."

We prayed together and boldly reclaimed this healing. It took time, but slowly, the pain went away and has not returned. I recently watched her run a 10K for fun—without pain.

In retrospect, I recognize I *believed* God in faith, *received* direction from Him to share with my daughter, *lived it* out by talking with her, and *gave it* by praying with her and sharing what was in my heart in that experience. It was the four-step action plan—*believe, receive, live it, give it*—summarized in one scenario. Not only did it help me experience a change through faith, but it also helped my daughter do the same.

My daughter went through some very tough years, but the blessing followed the pain. She believed in God when she was faced with contrary evidence. She is a great young woman who is strong in her faith and confident in her identity as God's daughter. We give God all glory and praise for that.

It was hard for us to understand how God could allow Lauren's pain to last for so long. You may be in a similar situation due to physical or emotional pain of some type. I realize many reading this may experience much tougher challenges.

Let me encourage you that God is with you, and He is always faithful.

> The Lord is good, a strong refuge when trouble comes. He is close to those who trust in Him.
>
> (Nahum 17:7 NLT)

Perhaps you are not in a struggle and wonder, "That is an awesome story, Brian, but what does it have to do with me?" Don't take this the wrong way, but you ask the wrong question! The question is, "What does this have to do with God?"

Remember, we need to move ourselves and our agendas out of the way.

Ask yourself, "What does this show me about God? What does this tell me about what God wants me to do?"

Here are some possible answers:

- God is faithful
- God heals
- God can heal by Himself or work through the care of medical personnel
- We need to resist the enemy through bold faith
- God honors our responses of active faith
- God wants us to communicate with Him and include Him in our daily lives
- We experience blessing and growth as the result of being faithful to God through painful times

We only need to look to the Bible to find more people that struggled and overcame painful situations:

- Abraham struggled with the ultimate obedience by being prepared to sacrifice Isaac, but God provided the ram in the bush. Abraham came out victoriously and ultimately full of more faith. God blessed Abraham through the promised future generations. (see Genesis 22)
- Jacob wrestled with God all night, received the name, Israel, as he struggled with God and humans and overcame. (see Genesis 32)
- Jesus overcame betrayal, the sin of the world, torture, and crucifixion on a cross for our sin. He defeated death and rose on the third day! (see John 20)

Jesus overcame so we can overcome!

I have said these things to you, that in me you may have peace. In the world you will have tribulation, but take heart; I have overcome the world.

(John 16:33 ESV)

As we live out our faith daily, we turn to the Lord in our struggles and pain. He will overcome for us as He did for Jacob, Joshua, Abraham, and our Savior, Jesus Christ.

Let us remember that blessing will follow the pain if we go through it God's way.

BIBLICAL EXAMPLE OF LIVING IT—APOSTLE PAUL

I can't think of anyone, other than Jesus, who lived out his faith more actively than the apostle Paul. He experienced a miraculous conversion on the road to Damascus and started his ministry immediately.

Paul was unstoppable. On one occasion, after he healed a crippled man, his haters stoned him within an inch of his life and dragged him outside of town:

> Then some Jews came from Antioch and Iconium and won the crowd over. They stoned Paul and dragged him outside the city, thinking he was dead. But after the disciples had gathered around him, he got up and went back into the city. The next day he and Barnabas left for Derbe.
>
> (Acts 14:19-20 NIV)

Not only was this a miracle physically, but it also showed incredible boldness on Paul's part!

Later in his ministry, Paul and his friend, Silas, were beaten and thrown into prison for healing people and sharing the gospel. Paul and Silas sang hymns and praised God from jail in the middle of the night. When the cell doors flew open from an earthquake, they didn't flee. They stayed at the prison, shared the gospel with the jailer, who then cleaned them up and invited them to his home. Paul and Silas led his whole family to Christ, baptized them, and ate dinner at the guard's house (see Acts 16:25-34).

No one could get to a guy like Paul. He was okay if he lived and okay if he died. Read what he wrote when imprisoned again:

> For to me, living means living for Christ, and dying is even better. But if I live, I can do more fruitful work for Christ. So I really don't know which is better. I'm torn between two desires: I long to go and be with Christ, which would be far better for me. But for your sakes, it is better that I continue to live.
>
> (Philippians 1:21-24 NLT)

Paul learned one of the real secrets of actively living out his faith—be content in all things and all environments. God was Paul's source of strength and had him in that place for a reason:

> "Not that I am speaking of being in need, for I have learned in whatever situation I am to be content. I know how to be brought low, and I know how to abound. In any and every circumstance, I have learned the secret of facing plenty and hunger, abundance and need. I can do all things through him who strengthens me"
>
> (Philippians 4:11-13 ESV)

Paul was content and bold for Christ in all situations. What a great example of *living it*!

LIVE IT BY BEING GENEROUS

> For where your treasure is there your heart will be also.
>
> (Matthew 6:21 ESV)

What else leads to active faith in Christ? Generosity. We need to be generous with our resources and our time. We must realize *everything* we have—relationships, possessions, time, health, and money—are the "Property of God." They are His. They came from Him and, when we die, they will continue to be used and moved around for His purposes here on earth.

When you give to a friend, neighbor, church, ministry, or relief effort, you open your hand and release to God what He gave you in the first place! (Remember the imagery earlier in the book about unclenching those hands?)

God puts breath in your lungs, supplies food and money for you to live and enjoy life. He gave you another day today. Shift your attitude and focus. You don't own anything; He owns it all. You are a temporary steward of your resources—let go of your grip on them, and God will honor that in a big way!

LIVE IT BY CHANGING YOUR DECISION-MAKING

I meet with my great friend Mike regularly for coffee. We talk about faith, family, and everything else. One day, we talked about a difficult decision he faced as a foster parent. It is important to Mike that faith is at the foundation of his life and choices. As we talked through his decision-making process, he said following God in his life seems to boil down to three things: (1) listening to God, (2) obeying God and, the foundation of everything, (3) trusting God.

We talked about getting into a rhythm of doing this every day in our lives. It takes practice to do these things. Mike and I both like baseball, so we compared this to the muscle memory developed practicing a baseball swing (or any other sporting activity). At first, when you learn or change the mechanics of your swing, it's uncomfortable and awkward. However, as you practice each part, you get better. It becomes more comfortable until it is part of your muscle memory. You do not have to think about your new swing path; you can focus on reacting to the pitch.

We develop our new muscle memory for decision making and living by listening, obeying, and trusting God, transforming our lives in the process. After all, we won't obey Him if we don't build trust in Him.

A NEW FILTER FOR OUR DECISIONS

What if we look at our decisions through a new lens?

Let's consider some examples of typical decisions we make:

- How should I spend my time this weekend?
- How do I handle this situation with my kids?
- Where should I live?
- Which job should I pursue?
- How will giving to the church affect my finances?
- Should I serve on this mission opportunity?

What's in it for me?

Often, this is the filter we use. It seems we are not willing to devote our time or money to an activity or purpose unless we sense there is something in it for us. It does not have to be a financial return or a new job. It could be recognition, praise, or approval. If we are honest, most of our decisions run through this filter at some level. Even something good, like giving to the church, can be this way. Are we giving out of a loving and obedient heart, so God can use it as He desires? Or, do we give to relieve a feeling of guilt, to get something from God, or others?

Jesus gave and acted without thinking, *"What's in it for me?"* Instead, He focused on that which brought glory to His Father:

After Jesus said this, he looked toward heaven and prayed:

"Father, the hour has come. Glorify your Son, that your Son may glorify you. For you granted him authority over all people that he might give eternal life to all those you have given

him. Now this is eternal life: that they know you, the only true God, and Jesus Christ, whom you have sent. I have brought you glory on earth by finishing the work you gave me to do."

(John 17:1-4 NIV)

So, how can we bring glory to God and point others to Him in our everyday lives? Perhaps, we could try a new filter for our decisions—*What's in it for God?*

As an individual, family member, or leader of an organization, we have a responsibility to be wise. However, we do not have to be wise all by ourselves. We can consult God for wisdom. We can "walk by faith and not by sight" (2 Corinthians 5:7 ESV).

God does not seek to harm us, but instead has plans to give us hope and a future (see Jeremiah 29:11). If we want to experience this hope and future that God has for us, we cannot think, "What's in it for me?"

Instead, we need to think, "What's in it for Him?" By Him, I mean God and the advancement of His purposes. By Him, I also refer to others. What's in it for your family members or friends, your brothers, and sisters in Christ? What's in it for the lost?

This focus shift is hard for everyone. As a husband and father, I feel the pressure of being a provider, financially wise, and responsible with my time. But, first, I am a son of God and a follower of Jesus. I want to be a Christ-imitator. And Christ did not ask, "What's in this for me?" Instead, He acted to bring glory to God through love for God and others.

Let's try new filters for our decisions. We apply these filters to how we spend our time, our money, actions toward others, and internal motivations. Here are some examples:

Fill a few hours of your free time: "Does this move me closer to God or farther away?"

Make a big career move: "Which decision is more likely to bring glory to God?"

Spend discretionary income: "What's in it for Him?"

Applying these filters helps us:

➢ Activate our faith in God seven days a week
➢ Love others the way Jesus did
➢ See what God wants for us and be more aligned with Him
➢ Focus on imitating Jesus, and not culture

God loves us. He is for us and not against us. God created us and blessed us with everything we have. He owns it all, including the blessings and the struggles. When we realize we don't own anything, we learn to love and live the way Jesus did. We are more likely to think, "What's in it for Him?" when we make decisions in our lives.

LIVE IT BY FORGIVING OTHERS

I have heard it said that forgiveness is more for the person doing the forgiving than the one forgiven. After all, if you hold a grudge against someone, it eats away at you more than them. When you forgive them, you will be amazed at the relief in your life, as well as the great blessing it will be for them.

I experienced this firsthand. My single mom raised me from the time I was three years old. My dad lived in another city, and I did not interact with him more than once or twice a year. When I was forty-eight, God put it on my heart to visit my father (a five-hour trip) and tell him I love him and forgive him.

I drove to my dad's for a visit. As the day went on, there was no natural opportunity for the talk that I wanted to have with him. So, I decided to do it. Finally, at the very end of the day, I took my dad aside in the restaurant parking lot and talked to him.

I said, "Dad, I believe God told me to come here today for a couple of reasons. First, He wanted me to tell you about how He's been active in my life."

My dad responded, "Active? I'd say he's taken over."

I replied, "That's the way I want it." Then, I looked my dad in the eyes and said, "I also want you to know I love you and forgive you," and I meant it.

He said, "I love you, too. I thought we were fine."

I believe my forgiveness impacted him, but it wasn't an earth-shattering reaction. Our relationship is still quite distant. We still have work to do, with God's help.

Nonetheless, I will never forget that two-minute talk. On the drive home, I felt relief, release, and freedom from a lifetime of pain I had in that area. It was all gone. By obeying God and forgiving my dad, God released the freedom He wanted me to experience.

Although my dad seemed somewhat touched for a moment, I was not sure about any impact until I talked with my brother later that year. He said Dad told him about my visit and its effect on him. Maybe my dad experienced the same freedom I did.

God does some of His best work through repentance and forgiveness. Forgiveness is something we are called to do. We are supposed to repent and seek forgiveness, as well as offer forgiveness to others. The apostle Paul reminded the Colossians of this in his letter to them:

> *Bear with each other and forgive one another if any of you has a grievance against someone. Forgive as the Lord forgave you.*
>
> *(Colossians 3:13 NIV)*

LIVE IT BY LOVING UNCONDITIONALLY

The most important way we can *live it* is to love others. People recognize we are followers of Christ by how we love others. You can praise and worship, be in a small group, and serve at your church, but if you don't show love to others, you're not *living it.*

> *A new command I give you: Love one another. As I have loved you, so you must love one another. By this everyone will know that you are my disciples, if you love one another.*
>
> *(John 13:34-35 NIV)*

We need to love unconditionally, the way Jesus did. We know we won't ever do this as well as Jesus, the perfect standard, but that doesn't mean we are not called to do it. Unconditional love starts in our home and spreads from there.

My mom was wonderful at this. Unconditional love was her best and most pervasive characteristic. During my process of writing this book, my mom passed on to be with the Lord in heaven. At her memorial service, my brother Bill shared these words about mom:

> Mom's greatest gift to others was her love. You knew she loved you, unconditionally. She really enjoyed her grandkids. She loved going to their games, attending school presentations, cooking together, watching movies, and making snacks. She always tried to make her house a fun place for kids. When I was growing up, most of my friends called her Mother Goose and enjoyed visiting with her. One of her traditions with everyone in the family was to call them on their birthday and sing, usually very early in the morning. We are all going to miss those birthday wake-up calls, but we pray that you are with Jesus now, breathing easier and no longer suffering.

We benefit significantly from God's forgiveness and unconditional love for us. If we truly repent and ask forgiveness from God, we know He forgives our sins. Are we doing the same for those in our life? For those closest to us, as well as our coworkers and neighbors? Sometimes it's easier to show love and forgiveness at a church small group or on a mission trip than it is with our own families. I know; I am guilty of not doing so many times.

Reflect on this and see if there is room for improvement. Loving and forgiving others, including those in our own families, is a crucial way we *live it*.

BROTHER LARRY REESE—AUTHOR, TEACHER, PASTOR, FRIEND

Brother Larry Reese, the man to whom I dedicated this book, was my teacher in discipleship school. Here's the thing about Brother Larry: He loves everybody unconditionally. He truly cares about others and demonstrates the love of Christ. He mentors them, disciples them, teaches them, and cooks sweet potato pie for them.

An author and ministry leader for over thirty years, Brother Larry is the Pastor of Discipleship at our local church, which is a tremendous blessing for us! He spends many hours every day with the Lord. Throughout his life, he's developed an intimate relationship with God.

I believe Brother Larry is the closest thing to Jesus that I will meet this side of heaven. He devotes his life to God's work and helps others do the same. That's *Living It*!

ACTIVATE YOUR FAITH—LIVE IT

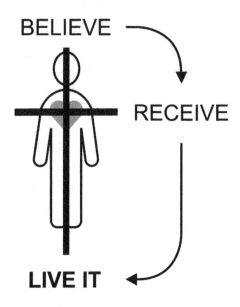

LIVE IT

We focus our hearts and minds on God, but ultimately, we live out our faith daily to experience real change in our lives and the lives of others. We put our faith into action.

LIVE IT THROUGH PRAYER

Fear is not my God
Safety is not my God
Comfort is not my God
Money is not my God
Approval of others is not my God

You, heavenly Father, are my God
You supply all my needs
You love me forever
I give this day to you. Not my will, but yours be done. Amen.

TIP: If you do not have a regular prayer life, try this: set your phone timer and pray for three minutes every day for a week. Once it becomes part of your routine, increase it to four minutes, and so on.

LIVE IT THROUGH THE BIBLE

[Read Luke 22: 39-65, focusing on this verse]

> *And he withdrew from them about a stone's throw, and knelt down and prayed, saying, "Father, if you are willing, remove this cup from me. Nevertheless, not my will, but yours, be done"*

> (Luke 22:41-42 ESV)

This passage speaks about a time of great pain for Jesus. How was He faithful through it?

How can you live out your faith, even more than you have already, through your painful situations? (examples: physical illness or pain, a problem with a boss or coworker, family pain)

LIVE IT THROUGH RELATIONSHIPS

Pick one or more of the following scenarios. Check off what you do and talk about it with a close friend.

Forgiveness

- ☐ Think about someone you have a grudge against. After praying sincerely about it, call that person and tell them you forgive them. Be specific.

Generosity

- ☐ Increase your giving at your local church.
- ☐ Pay for someone's meal at the fast food counter.
- ☐ Leave a $20 tip on a restaurant bill that is lower than that.

Love

- ☐ Think of someone you don't usually show love to and show them God's love in a practical way. (examples: a homeless person, a competitor at work.)

LIVE IT THROUGH A RENEWED MIND

Post this *Living It* chart where you will see it daily. Try to follow it, and quiz yourself once in a while on how you did that day.

LIVING IT	NOT LIVING IT
Focus is on God	Focus is on me
Faith, not fear	Fear, not faith
God's way	The world's way
Joy	Frustration
Peace	Anxiety
Generosity	Greed
Loving unconditionally	Loving with conditions
Full surrender to God	Partial surrender to God
Gratitude	Wanting what's owed to me
Listening and obeying how God tells me how to live	Asking God to bless the way I want to live

LIVE IT: JOURNAL TIME

Look at your decisions this week through a new lens: *What's in it for Him?*

☐ In your journal, list at least one decision you made this week intentionally considering "What's in it for Him" instead of "What's in it for me?" List the result.

(Don't list an easy answers like *going to church*. Put real and practical decisions here, such as how your family spent free time, a decision you made with your money, a child-raising decision, etc.)

1. _____

2. _____

3. _____

Living it is about putting God first, pursuing Him with our whole heart, and imitating Christ through forgiving others and loving them unconditionally. This pursuit leads to living out our faith actively in our decision-making, generosity, and faithfulness amid pain and struggles.

Want to take it to the next level? Join an online small group, take the Changed Through Faith Action Plan course, or sign up for faith development coaching at ctfaith.com.

CHAPTER 7
GIVE IT

For you have been called to live in freedom, my brothers and sisters. But don't use your freedom to satisfy your sinful nature. Instead, use your freedom to serve one another in love.

(Galatians 5:13 ESV)

In this final step of the plan, *giving it,* we start and end with our role model, Jesus. The greatest giver to ever walk the earth, Jesus was the only person who ever lived who did not sin. Therefore, He gave out of a pure heart from a place of absolute love and compassion.

As we discussed in the last chapter, it is not only our activity and behavior God is concerned with but also our heart and motives. To learn how to *give it*—our faith, love, encouragement, time, talents, and treasures—we learn from the way Jesus gave to others.

Jesus gave by:

> ➢ Loving
> ➢ Serving
> ➢ Teaching
> ➢ Obeying

Why should we strive to give like Jesus?

Because if we only *Believe*, *Receive*, and *Live* our faith, we grow and benefit *ourselves*, but do not *help others* do the same. And besides, we are called to *give it* by Jesus:

> *"Go therefore and make disciples of all nations, baptizing them in the name of the Father and of the Son and of the Holy Spirit, teaching them to observe all that I have commanded you. And behold, I am with you always, to the end of the age."*
>
> *(Matthew 28:19-20 ESV)*

GIVING YOUR FAITH

How do you give your faith?

We cannot give our personal faith to someone, but we can encourage them to have faith in God by relating our story and treating them well.

CHARLEY—SHARE YOUR STORY

My friend, Charley, is one of the most loving and down-to-earth guys I've ever met. Charley is a straight-talker from the Bronx, NY, who isn't ashamed to love Jesus. The first time I met Charley, I shook his hand, and he said, "I'm Charley, a sober drunk who loves to help the least and the lost." And the cool part is that's exactly what he does! He will gladly share all the mistakes he's made, if it will save you from making one, and help you get closer to Jesus.

One day, we were talking about how to defend our Christian faith when confronted by others. Charley said, "You may be able to argue with me on details of the Bible, but you can't argue with my story, because it's *my story* of what Jesus did for me."

Charley's right. Jesus gave us all a story, which is continually developing into a greater one. Do you like to listen to a preacher tell a good story? Aren't we attracted to a good story in a book or movie? Jesus used stories all the time, called parables, to teach his disciples.

Guess what? You have a story! How did you accept Jesus as your Savior? If you haven't done that yet, what is the story that's holding you back? What have you overcome because of Jesus?

Do you think Lazarus had a story to share? Jesus raised him from the dead! (Read the story in the Gospel of John, chapter 11.) I can picture him at his kid's sandlot baseball game with the other dads, trying to bring it up nonchalantly:

> What a great night, huh fellows? The other team seems to be giving up a lot of walks. Speaking of walking, did I mention I'm walking right now because Jesus brought me back from the dead?

There are many places, times, and ways to share your faith. Your story encourages others and draws them closer to God.

EVANGELISM

I was scared of the word *evangelism* because I didn't know what it meant. When I finally figured it out, I thought evangelism was for the pastor or holy people to do. I thought, "I'll let *them* tell others about the gospel, whatever that means."

As time went on, God radically transformed my heart and life. I am compelled to tell others about it, so they experience the same freedom, joy, and peace that took me thirty years to discover. I want others to get there more quickly than I did. God does the transforming, but I can be obedient in any plans He has for me to carry out.

Our stories show the power of God to transform and heal. They attract others to God because they build faith.

So, how can you evangelize? Share your story.

It is a great and easy first step toward *giving it.* Let's look at how we give like Jesus through:

> ➤ *Loving* with compassion and acceptance
> ➤ *Serving* with our time, talents, and treasure
> ➤ *Teaching* as mentors, friends, and parents
> ➤ *Obeying* as children of God

GIVE BY LOVING

We give by loving as Jesus loved. He accepted everyone and had compassion for peoples' struggles. He always pointed them toward God. Bob Goff, author of *Love Does*, puts it this way, "Love everybody, always."

How can we do this?

LOVING THROUGH PRAYER

I asked God to show me how to love others and see them as He does. It did not happen instantly. I am still not very good at it, but I am better. How did I get better at it? I prayed it and then practiced it. I reminded myself as I read the Gospels and saw Jesus doing it time after time. Eventually, it started to sink in and transform my heart and mind.

> *Do not conform to the pattern of this world, but be trans-formed by the renewing of your mind. Then you will be able to test and approve what God's will is—his good, pleasing and perfect will.*
>
> *(Romans 12:2 NIV)*

LOVING YOUR FAMILY

A word of caution: Don't be surprised if the first people God puts in your heart to love are the people with whom you have baggage. It might be family members or someone with whom you have a grudge. God knows if you love them as He does, you gain the confidence to do that with everyone else.

God did this in my life when He put it on my heart to visit my dad, share my faith with him, and tell him, "I love you and forgive you." As I shared earlier, my mom raised me. My parents divorced when I was three, and my mom moved us to a different state. So when God brought this up while driving down the road, I thought, "Really, God? I hardly ever see him. We're not that close. Can I start with someone else?"

Right then, out of my driver's side window was a massive high-way billboard advertisement with a father and son, with the quote, "Do it for dad!" Are you kidding me? I got the point. I pointed up to God, smiled, and said, "Nice one!"

Eventually, I obeyed and drove the five hours to do what God told me to do. When I forgave my dad, all the bitterness I carried for years melted away. I have a new compassion and love for him and see him as a brother in Christ who needs God as much as I do.

GOD'S LOVE IS FOR EVERYONE

I remember an occasion when I was eating lunch in a restaurant with a family member who was being critical of others. I said, "Look around this restaurant. You see everyone here? Jesus died for them, too. Each one. He loves every person the same way He loves you."

While that perspective made an immediate impact, it did not come from my regular *Brian* thoughts; it came from a renewed mind. God renews your heart and mind when you build your relationship with Him through prayer and reading the Bible.

LOVING BY LISTENING

For twenty-two years, I was a school teacher. I did a lot of talking, but I also did some important listening. Through the years, I had many meetings with troubled students and angry parents. I found that listening was the best strategy in these situations. The parents and students wanted to be heard. They wanted to know that their thoughts and feelings mattered. While we did not always agree on solutions, listening worked to calm and diffuse difficult situations.

Many of us are eager to tell others our problems, get advice, and fix other people's situations. There is nothing wrong with those activities. However, if we don't decide to *intentionally and actively listen*, then we probably won't. When we do listen actively, we position ourselves to connect with people at a deeper level with more compassion, which allows us to give to people as God teaches us.

GIVE BY SERVING

Jesus loved, served, and encouraged. So should we. When you read the heading *serving*, did you automatically think of mission trips and church service projects? Those are undoubtedly valuable and worthwhile ways to serve. However, let's look at serving on a more practical and straightforward level.

We need to serve and encourage others with a heart of love, *expecting nothing in return*. Easier said than done.

> We need to serve and encourage others with a heart of love, expecting nothing in return.

DENNY — "THE CATALYST"

Denny is phenomenal at *giving it* through serving. I call Denny "The Catalyst" because he gets things done. Denny takes action to serve others, especially for God's Kingdom. He loves to connect purposes and people. Here is a simple example of Denny in action.

One summer day, while visiting Denny in his office, we talked about faith and family. As the discussion continued, I told him how my son recently moved back home from college and was considering transferring to a local community college that fall. He needed a new setting to continue his college academics and baseball career. As our talk wound down, Denny asked for my son's phone number. I gave it to him and then asked why he needed it. It turns out, that during our conversation, "The Catalyst" had jumped on our local community college website, filled out the student interest form on Jordan's behalf, and contacted the coach right there on his office computer, without me even knowing it.

Guess who showed up at my son's game the very next day? That's right, the coach. It turns out his summer team played on the field right next to ours. Imagine my son's surprise when the coach came up, responding to "my son's request!"

Denny is excellent at *giving it* by actively serving others. Think about the last time you scheduled a lunch or coffee appointment with a friend. Were you trying to *give* or *get* from the meeting? When my son was young and having trouble with sharing, I made him a simple sign for his room. Here is what it said:

"What can I ~~get~~...give?"

You give by being a great listener. Spend time this week encouraging others through texts, a lunch, or even an old-fashioned phone call to listen and encourage someone, without wanting anything in return. I guarantee you will be blessed if you do!

GIVE WHAT YOU HAVE

You cannot give what you don't have. Take an inventory of your time, skills, and resources. Can you leverage some of your time to mentor a friend? Can you use your natural talents to expand the reach of the gospel? Can you cut back on expenses and reroute that money to God's work?

EXAMPLE OF GIVING IT—A SPECIAL GIFT RECEIVED

One of my passions is serving as director of a nonprofit organization called Changed Through Faith Ministries. We help fathers and their families grow closer to God and each other.

We receive gifts from people who generously give their resources. On one occasion, God blessed our ministry in a remarkable way through someone who understood about *giving it* and acted on it.

I returned home from a trip to Illinois, where I visited a friend who opened a new facility for his ministry. This friend gave $40 monthly to our ministry faithfully, but, after the visit, I told him to suspend his giving to us and put that money into his new ministry.

Upon my return, I went to our organization's post office box to collect the mail. As I opened the letter, I received a surprise donation check for $480 from a man I knew, but who moved away several months before. We had only one conversation about our ministry before he moved.

Amazingly, this check replaced the exact amount of annual donations from the friend I told to steer his contribution toward his ministry! It was a meaningful gift to our organization, and an example of how giving through our resources can have much more impact than we often know.

BIBLICAL EXAMPLE OF GIVING IT—PETER & JOHN

When you give what you have, amazing things happen not only to whom you gave, but also to others. Consider the following story from the book of Acts in the Bible.

> *Now Peter and John were going up to the temple at the hour of prayer, the ninth hour. And a man lame from birth was being carried, whom they laid daily at the gate of the temple that is called the Beautiful Gate to ask alms of those entering the temple. Seeing Peter and John about to go into the temple, he asked to receive alms. And Peter directed his gaze at him, as did John, and said, "Look at us." And he fixed his attention on them, expecting to receive something from them. But Peter said, "I have no silver and gold, but what I do have I give to you. In the name of Jesus Christ of Nazareth, rise up and walk!" And he took him by the right hand and raised him up, and immediately his feet and ankles were made strong. And leaping up, he stood and began to walk, and entered the temple with them, walking and leaping and praising God.*

> *And all the people saw him walking and praising God, and recognized him as the one who sat at the Beautiful Gate of the temple, asking for alms. And they were filled with wonder and amazement at what had happened to him.*

> *(Acts 3:1-10 ESV)*

When I wrote earlier, "you can't give your faith," maybe I was wrong! Peter relied on his faith in God to heal this man, and God did. Not only that, but when Peter gave what he had, the other people around him experienced an increase in their faith.

Peter and John then took the opportunity to teach the people. The religious leaders got upset and threw them in jail, but not before five thousand people came to believe in Jesus Christ!

You can't control the reaction of others when you give what you have. The recipients may be grateful or greedy. Your family may say you're nuts. Some of your friends may question your motives. Here's what I know: Peter and John did not stop to think, "I wonder what others will think of me." They acted in bold faith and gave healing prayer to this lame beggar.

LOOK FOR THE NEED

A big key to serving is recognizing the need. Listening to God and others is part of discerning the need. Take the focus off yourself. God teaches you to do this, and He shows you what needs to be done if you trust Him and spend time with Him. God won't necessarily show you the need by booming it in a loud voice from a thundercloud, "Thou shalt taketh dinner to your sick neighbor today!"

Simply be vigilant. Look for a need to be met. Expect it; then meet it.

NICK — A STUDENT OF GIVING IT

When I was a teacher, Nick, a student, was better at this than anyone. He had an uncanny ability to see unspoken needs and meet them; all without being told to do it by a teacher. If Nick came in the music classroom and the equipment wasn't set up for jazz band, he set it up. If something was happening in the chapel space later that day that required sound equipment, Nick set it up. If someone needed the sheet music for worship band rehearsal, he got it to them. Nick did this every day without anyone ever telling him to do it.

Nick exhibited servant leadership. He made others around him better and served them with humility. Sounds like someone else I know—our role model, Jesus.

Jesus saw needs all around Him, whether it was healing people or feeding five thousand people from two loaves and five fish. Serve by recognizing the need and then giving what you have to meet it. Remember, you don't have to wait. You can activate your faith today by giving daily. God can bless your obedience and multiply its effect.

SERVING THROUGH PRAYER

Jesus served through prayer. We learn from our role model and imitate Him by praying for others.

In John 17, this is very evident. It's one of my favorite chapters in the Bible. The first time I read it was in a park where the following words jumped out at me:

> *"My prayer is not for them alone. I pray also for those who will believe in me through their message."*
>
> *(John 17:20 NIV)*

Then it dawned on me, *Jesus prayed for me* to His Father two thousand years before I even got here! Does that surprise you? I was stunned. Jesus, God in the flesh, prayed intently and intentionally for you and me. If He did it, we should do it.

When you tell someone, "I'll pray for you," do it right then, on the spot. You may catch them off guard or make them a bit uncomfortable, but in most cases, they appreciate it.

PRAYING AT THE DRIVE-THROUGH

Occasionally, when I pay at the drive-through window, I say, "Hi, how are you? I like to pray when I drive. Is there anything you need prayer for?" They almost always answer with something besides, "No."

One time, someone asked me to pray for a new job for them! On another occasion, the worker leaned out the window, told me he had a baby on the way, and asked me to pray for that.

They usually have a name tag, so after they tell you their prayer request, say, "Thank you, Maggie. I will pray for that today." People appreciate that you recognize and care about their struggles enough to ask and to pray for them. I believe in the power of prayer.

GIVE BY TEACHING

Jesus *gave it* by teaching with actions without words, with shrewdness and boldness. He taught with long sermons, short sermons, parables, and even one-liners. Whether it was teaching individuals or groups, Jesus helped people stretch and grow in their faith in God.

We have many opportunities to teach others what we have learned in our walk with God. Regardless of where we are on the journey, there is someone who needs to hear about where you are right now. We give through mentoring, parenting, and being a great friend. It is most effective if we do it intentionally and actively.

MENTORING

As we *believe*, *receive*, and *live out* our faith, it is our responsibility to *give it* away, to pour into others. I like to teach through writing and speaking, but my greatest joy is helping people one-on-one. Several years ago, I began intentional coffee meetings with people that (1) I mentor, (2) mentor me, and (3) have a balance each way. I have one or two friends in each category. These are people who are mature in their Christian faith. All of us go through struggles, and nothing is off limits. We are there to learn, teach, and share real life stuff.

If you are not in any intentional mentoring relationships as a giver, start now. Some of the most significant fruit comes from these types of relationships.

PARENTING

Your home is the prime mission field and place to give away your faith. Do you think that's your church's job? Even if your family went to church every single week, that's only 52 hours a year in church vs. 365 hours you spend with your kids at the rate of one hour per day. Your influence with your kids isn't only to love and discipline; it's to lead them spiritually. After all, disciple is in the word discipline.

FRIENDSHIP

You can teach your friends, maybe not by preaching at them, but by how you live your life. If they notice positive changes in you because of God, that's a great thing. Can people tell you've been hanging out with Jesus? It should be evident—not necessarily as a result of you telling them—but because of the way you live your life, as you grow closer to God.

GIVE BY OBEYING

When we give ourselves and our faith to others, we must obey God in it. We can't make up a bunch of good stuff to do and expect fulfillment if we aren't following God's lead. Jesus was always in contact with His Father. Here is how the Gospel of John records it:

> Jesus gave them this answer: "Very truly I tell you, the Son can do nothing by himself; he can do only what he sees his Father doing, because whatever the Father does the Son also does.
>
> (John 5:19 NIV)

To obey means to yield to God's plan and will for our lives. Here is a Biblical example of sincere obedience:

> And he said to them, "Follow me, and I will make you fishers of men." Immediately they left their nets and followed him.
>
> (Matthew 4:19-20 ESV)

God has things for you to do through loving, teaching, and serving, which requires obedience.

Our job is to obey. The result is God's job.

NO AGENDA EXCEPT GOD'S

When we give to others by serving them or mentoring them, we shouldn't have an agenda. When we give by starting a ministry or going on a mission trip, we can't base it on our desires. To give as Jesus did, the Holy Spirit leads and motivates through care and compassion for other people. In that way, we operate by God's agenda in active faith.

When we yield to God as leader of our lives, we give to others because He leads us. He rewires our hearts and thoughts to be more like His. As a result, we don't give *to look good* or get something for ourselves.

I know that sounds like a perfect standard because it is. Jesus was perfect. He is also our role model. If you were learning to be a top-level quarterback, you would imitate the best. Just because you may not be the number one draft choice, doesn't mean you don't try your best!

BECAUSE JESUS DID

Why should we give our time, talents, treasures, faith, love, and encouragement to others? Because Jesus did.

Why should we give it in a posture of obedience to God? Because Jesus did.

A discussion of obediently giving is not complete without reminding ourselves that Jesus gave it all in obedience to the Father. The night before He was to go to the cross for our sins, He prayed:

Father, if you are willing, take this cup from me; yet not my will, but yours be done.

(Luke 22:42 NIV)

Jesus taught us how to give in many ways, but none more so than giving up His life for us so we could experience salvation and everlasting life.

ONE VITAL INGREDIENT TO THE PLAN

The Changed Through Faith Action Plan steps contain many ways to live out active faith through our relationship with God and others.

> ➤ We learn to *Believe* in God and His promises.

> ➤ We learn to *Receive* God's truths, love and forgiveness that comes through a relationship with Jesus, and the power it has to transform our hearts and lives.

> ➤ We learn how to *Live* out our faith actively.

> ➤ We learn how to *Give* our faith and love away to others as we serve them.

However, these actions will not lead to a consistently fulfilling and extraordinary life in Christ, without one crucial ingredient: Accepting *"It's not about me."*

Jesus taught this when he said:

"If you cling to your life, you will lose it; but if you give up your life for me, you will find it."

(Matthew 10:39 NLT)

We cannot give freely the way God wants us to if we focus on WIIFM—*What's In It For Me*. Jesus did not teach us that. He taught us to serve and give selflessly:

> *Sitting down, Jesus called the Twelve and said, "Anyone who wants to be first must be the very last, and the servant of all."*
>
> (Mark 9:35 NIV)

BEN — FROM GETTING TO GIVING

Ben's life changed through faith. During this transformation, Ben switched his focus from himself to God.

Here is how he described what happened from our interview:

> It's been a journey. Christ changed me in so many ways, and the fact that He answers when we call is amazing.
>
> Before I dedicated my life to Christ, it was about me. I thought,
>
> - How much can I achieve?
> - How important can I become?
> - How popular can I be?
> - How can I look like the best compared to others?
>
> It was about me; that was the end goal. The goal was for me to be on the pedestal, people clapping.
>
> That's my mentality when God's out of the picture. I still fall into that mentality, but now I

have the Holy Spirit who checks me. And now that I follow God, my way of thinking shifted from being me-centered to God-centered.

When I embrace a repentant heart, recognizing that I can't do this alone, I'm in a vulnerable place. I need God in every area of my life, and I've been winning since I surrendered to God. There is nothing more real.

Now my goals are completely different. I want to serve God. I want God to be glorified not only through my testimony but also through other peoples' lives that I'm in contact with. I want to help people see how God is at work in their lives; that's my ultimate goal.

It's very simple: I want to get closer to God, and I want to help others to do the same thing.

GOD CHANGED MY FOCUS

I experienced this change of focus as well, but it took time. During a retreat a couple of years ago, I worked through a tough time. I asked God to show me the real reason for my turmoil, even though I knew I might not like it. About an hour or so later, after a time of prayer, reading, and reflecting, God prompted me to write this in my journal:

IT'S NOT ABOUT BRIAN

As I got to my name, I was going to write the word *me*. But God made it clear to write my name and make it *personal*.

Earlier that year, God taught me, "It's not about me." But this time, He called me by name and made it even more personal.

Several years earlier, God gave me some ideas about a ministry I started. The revelation that none of it was about me helped me realize I tried to *own* the vision that God showed me, which is why I experienced so much frustration. I realized that taking ownership of God's vision is much different than:

- Walking toward God's vision, not yours
- Being part of a vision but not owning it
- Stewarding a vision
- His plan isn't about me as much as it's about Him!

There is only one way His plan and vision are about me, and that's in my *obedience*. I had to take my focus off myself. I thought and prayed, "How do I put *me* on the cross and in the tomb, and raise Jesus in my place?"

The answer? Through *obedience*. To do that, without experiencing confusion and frustration, I had to obey in a way that was joyful, privileged, and not about me.

Staying focused on God, helps me remember

- It's not about me
- It's about His vision
- It's about His love and redemption of His hurting people

Once I stopped thinking God owed me something and realized this life is about Him and His plan, I started *Believing, Receiving, Living It,* and *Giving It* on a whole new level!

ACTIVATE YOUR FAITH—GIVE IT

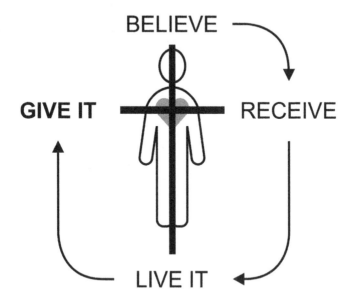

GIVE IT

This faith journey is not for our growth and benefit alone; it is also for others. God wants us to give generously with our time, talents, treasures, compassion, and Christ-like love.

GIVE IT THROUGH PRAYER

God, I am blessed by Your love and forgiveness. I am blessed by people You sent and by Your provision. Help me be obedient and active in sharing it with others. Help me to listen to how You want me to give Your love away and then do it. Help me to see and love others the way that You do. Amen.

GIVE IT THROUGH THE BIBLE

Then Peter said, "Silver or gold I do not have, but what I do have I give you. In the name of Jesus Christ of Nazareth, walk."

(Acts 3:6 NIV)

☐   What do you have that you can give? (List a time, talent, resource, etc.)

☐   Look at the verses in this chapter. Pick one you like and give it to another person, even someone in your family. You can text it, write in on a sticky note, email it, etc.

GIVE IT THROUGH RELATIONSHIPS

Check the left box for any of these you plan to do this week. In one week, come back to this page and check the right box if you did it. Keep at it for several more tries until you check all the boxes on the left and the right!

☐   GIVE: To God (e.g., time)   ☐
☐   GIVE: To your neighbor   ☐
☐   GIVE: To your kids   ☐
☐   GIVE: To your spouse   ☐
☐   GIVE: To your friend   ☐

As you give it through relationships, remember to

➢   Build up instead of tear down
➢   Encourage instead of discourage
➢   Love instead of hate

➢ Accept instead of reject
➢ Give instead of take

GIVE IT THROUGH A RENEWED MIND

Below are some ways Jesus gave away His love and faith. This week try to renew your mind through these ways of thinking and acting.

Loving with compassion and acceptance

☐ Is there someone in your family you can love with more compassion? Demonstrate that to them this week.

Serving with our time, talents, and treasures

☐ What are some things you are good at?

_____

☐ Where can you cut back on expenses and reroute that money to God's work?

_____

Teaching as mentors, friends, and parents

☐ How can you leverage some of your time to mentor a friend in need?

_____

GIVE IT: JOURNAL TIME

Obeying as children of God

- ☐ What is a thought or idea from God that won't go away?

  _____

- ☐ Discuss it with one or two trusted Christian friends. With affirmation in place, take one step toward that thought, change, or idea this month. Reflect on the decision and the results in your journal.

Ready to take it to the next level? Join an online small group, take the Changed Through Faith Action Plan course, or sign up for faith development coaching at ctfaith.com.

CHAPTER 8
TIME TO RESPOND

I drove to work one morning at a time when I was going through a difficult season of life. As I approached a particular intersection, I remembered a great man I knew named Robby, who had lived nearby. He lost his battle with cancer a few months before. He was forty-eight.

Robby loved the Lord, his family, and others. In a previous job, Robby recruited and trained me to be part of an industry-leading company. He was among the national sales leaders year after year. He was hard-working and loved by many. Robby handled his illness with faith, dignity, love, and service, even teaching others life lessons through a daily blog.

As I pulled away from that intersection, I thought, "What would I do if I received that diagnosis?" My immediate response was, "I would tell as many people about Jesus as I could, as fast as I could." The next thought, without hesitation, was

"What are you waiting for?"

There was no doubt in my mind or heart, then or now, that was God's response.

Now, it was my turn to *respond to God.*

So, I did. I decided God was right. After all, why would I wait for a diagnosis or some other traumatic catalyst? There was no reason to wait. I started to activate my faith. Even though my miraculous healing in the doctor's office hadn't occurred yet, and I was still in the midst of significant struggles, I moved closer to God. Ultimately, I changed through faith in God, and so did my life. As I looked back after many years, I discovered this change in me came through responding to God actively by *Believing, Receiving, Living It,* and *Giving It.*

Now that you know the steps of the plan, *it's up to you to act.* It's time to *respond* to this book, to God, to your situation, to your circumstances, and *activate* your faith on a new level. No matter where you start, you can always progress further.

Any step is significant. A small step is a step as much as a big one. Reading any page of this book is a step. Doing an Activate Your Faith item is a step. Engaging with others going through the book online because you need hope and encouragement is a step.

Taking *any* action is better than not.

ARE YOU WAITING?

If your home had an air quality problem that detrimentally affected your health, you wouldn't wait to fix it or move. If you had a promotion opportunity at work that was right on all levels and you had to decide now, you wouldn't wait. If you had a child with a serious illness and the right treatment was available, you would quickly get it.

So, when it comes to how we live our lives each day, why do we settle for mediocrity and life happening to us when God has more for us? Do we not see it is urgent we experience a meaningful life full of peace and joy, instead of a life of frustration, lacking in meaning and purpose, because we don't follow God's ways and plans for us?

You ask, "What do I risk by waiting to live the life God is calling me to live?"

In my life, I risked my health, my marriage, and healthy relationships with my kids. I risked not helping others the way God wired me to help them. Ultimately, I risked missing the chance to live out the purpose God put me on this earth to fulfill.

If I had continued on my own path and ignored God's call to follow Him fully, I would have destroyed my marriage, my family, and my life. Not only that, I would have been miserable along the way and continued to make those around me miserable, affecting their daily lives as well.

How about you? Are you frustrated? Do you have secret areas of sin no one knows about? Do you struggle with idolizing the wrong things or with pride? Do you have some thorn that won't go away, is distracting you from living a joyful life, and is wearing you down mentally, physically, or spiritually?

Wherever you are, I encourage you to pause and do an honest self-examination of your life. Are you confident you are experiencing all God has for you? Are you walking in active faith with God every day, communicating with Him, listening to Him, experiencing His presence, and humbly following Him? If you are, that is awesome! You are responding to God with faith and obedience.

We all like a sure thing. Often, we wait to proceed because we lack certainty in the outcome of our actions. We're not sure it's going to work out, so we delay starting.

Suppose God says to you,

> I'm waiting for you to follow Me, to respond to Me, to spend time with Me. I gave you the ability to believe in Me and to have faith. I love you with an everlasting and steadfast love. I forgave you when you made mistakes and said you were sorry. I gave you my Son, Jesus. I want you to respond and follow Me. Learn and follow My plan for your life, as it offers abundantly more peace and joy than you would ever know without Me. I will supply your needs if you seek first the kingdom of God. Follow Me. What are you waiting for?

How would you respond? Are you hesitant? God says you do not have to get your act together first, get the new job, quit the addiction, find a spouse, go to a new church, start going to any church, or feel like it. Respond now. You can live a life that's changed through faith now.

RESPOND

God wants you to have faith in Him by responding to Him actively, no matter your circumstances or how you may be feeling. He gave us life. God gave us Jesus and the opportunity to live eternal and abundant life here on earth and in heaven. He gave us everything we have and everything we will ever have and need.

So, *what are you waiting for?* Respond to God through active faith.

I often say faith is a verb. I know it's not a verb, but we should live like it is. Faith lived out as an *action* is how we *respond* to God and His love for us. Every step of this action plan starts and ends with a deep-down, conviction-filled faith. It is an active response of faith.

Respond by *Believing.*

Respond by *Receiving.*

Respond by *Living It.*

Respond by *Giving It.*

God's faithfulness is awaiting your response.

Will you *respond?*

POSTLUDE

During the course of writing this book, my mother, Pam Goslee, passed away. The circumstances of her passing brought glory to God, not only because He spared her from a long period of severe suffering, but also because of what God did through His Word.

My mom's final day came quite suddenly, and I was not in town. My brother and I communicated by phone and, thankfully, he was able to reach me so I could say goodbye to her over the phone and reassure her of the great heaven that awaited her soon.

That was at around 6:00 a.m. Fifteen minutes later, like 300 million others around the world, I received that day's Bible verse, Matthew 6:25, through my YouVersion Bible app:

> *Therefore I tell you, do not be anxious about your life, what you will eat or what you will drink, nor about your body, what you will put on. Is not life more than food, and the body more than clothing?*

> *(Matthew 6:25 ESV)*

My mom's main struggles her entire life were with anxiety and worry. In her last days, she was concerned about what she was eating and the weight she was losing.

A few minutes after receiving that verse, I received a text from my brother that read, "Mom went to heaven at 6:25." To some, this might seem to be a coincidence, but it's not. It is *evidence*— Matthew 6:25 to 300 million people around the world!

God is real. He cares about us and our times of trouble. He moves mountains. With Him, all things are possible if we focus on things above.

He is in the business of changing lives through faith in Him.

And He wants to start right now with yours.

*   *   *

Do you need a change in your:

Outlook?
Shift it through faith.

Habits?
Break them through faith.

Beliefs?
Transform them through faith.

The time is now!

CHANGED THR⏻UGH FAITH

You've read the book, now experience the plan.

Join others and be encouraged today at CTFaith.com

The best way to respond and make a change is to take action. You started that through the *Activate Your Faith* sections at the ends of the chapters. Your next step to implement lasting change is to take the Changed Through Faith Action Plan course, join our small group program (online or in-person), or enroll in faith development coaching.

All participants completing these programs come away with a personalized Changed Through Faith Action Plan to apply to their lives.

Are you ready to respond? Join us today at ctfaith.com.

THE CHANGED THROUGH FAITH QUICK CHECK

Take our online assessment at ctfaith.com.

Ask a friend to join you as your CTFaith Quick Check Partner. Every week call each other and check in on these items.

1. BELIEVE
- ☐ How are you doing with *Believe*?
- ☐ Are you believing the promises and Word of God or the lies of culture and the enemy?
- ☐ Are you operating out of fear or faith?

2. RECEIVE
- ☐ How are you doing with *Receive*?
- ☐ Did you read the Bible at least three times this week?
- ☐ Have you listened to God quietly at least three times this week?
- ☐ Are you reading the Bible passively or actively *receiving* God's love, forgiveness, ideas, and plans?

3. LIVE IT
- ☐ How did you *Live It* this week?
- ☐ If people followed you with a news camera, would they see evidence of time spent with God?

4. GIVE IT
- ☐ Are you *Giving It* away?
- ☐ Have you given away time or money this week to someone who needed it and to your church?
- ☐ Did you share a personal story related to your faith this week and show unconditional love this week?

ABOUT THE AUTHOR

Brian Goslee is a follower of Jesus, husband, father, author, speaker, and coach. After twenty-three years in education, Brian founded and became Executive Director of Changed Through Faith Ministries, a nonprofit organization dedicated to helping fathers and their families grow closer to God and each other. The ministry hosts several faith-infused events throughout the year and provides other resources. Brian has a heart to serve God, serve others, and help them grow in their faith. Brian is active as a guest speaker. Contact him at brian@ctfaith.com and ctfaith.com.

PRAYER RESOURCES

REFLECTIONS ON HOW TO PRAY

In different seasons of my life, I sensed the Holy Spirit teaching me how to pray. The Holy Spirit reminds me to pray boldly, richly, and expectantly—with a full measure of faith. In other words, put my faith into action.

We are to pray as if we understand the power of whom we're praying to; praying in a way that is deeper, richer, and pours out more of ourselves. Take time not only to talk to God but also to listen to Him. Talk with God in a way you would with anyone else you love and respect!

BELIEVE

BELIEVER'S PRAYER OF SALVATION

If you do not yet believe in God and confess Jesus Christ as the Savior of your life, I invite you to do so right now. Pray this prayer:

Dear God, I admit I have sinned against You, and I need a Savior. I believe that Savior is Jesus Christ, Your Son, who came to earth, died on a cross for my sins, and on the third day rose from the dead. I choose to believe in Jesus as my Lord and follow You all the days of my life. Amen.

Congratulations! If you prayed that prayer and meant it in your heart, I encourage you to reach out to a Christian friend, a local church, or us to talk about your decision to follow Jesus Christ so you can receive some next steps! You can reach us at support@ctfaith.com.

DO YOU NEED TO RECOMMIT TO GOD?

Do you already believe in God the Father, Son, and Holy Spirit? Are you living it out? Do you need a *refresher* or a *boost* in your belief?

Pray this prayer and visit ctfaith.com for some biblically based next steps.

PRAYER TO RECOMMIT TO GOD

Lord, I believe in You and love You. I have sinned against you, and I turn from that sin and back toward You. Please forgive me. I recommit my life to You as Lord of my life, and I want to follow You all my days through my relationship with Jesus Christ, Your Son.

RECEIVE
REFLECTIONS ON PRAYING IN THE NAME OF JESUS

To pray in the name of Jesus means to pray, "Thy will be done" and to mean it, regardless of the consequences, whether it matches up with what you want in your flesh, in your life, or this culture.

To pray in the name of Jesus means to believe what God tells you, even before seeing physical evidence come to fruition.

Praying in the name of Jesus means believing in, and relying on, the power of the Holy Spirit.

Praying in the name of Jesus means worshiping Him, thanking Him, and experiencing His peace and joy, regardless of our circumstances.

Praying in the name of Jesus means pouring out our heart to Him, praying fervently, honestly, and expectantly.

PRAYER ABOUT PURPOSE

Lord, I want to understand my role in Your plan with clarity and understanding that can only come from You. I want to fulfill that role to Your glory, with absolute faith, and with love and boldness. Amen.

PRAYER ABOUT PROVISION

You are my God

Fear is not my God
Safety is not my God
Comfort is not my God
My paycheck is not my God
Approval of others is not my God

You, heavenly Father, are my God
You supply all my needs
You love me forever! Amen.

PRAYER TO THE HOLY SPIRIT

Holy Spirit, You live inside me.

Let Your wisdom take over in place of my thinking.
Let Your Spirit of faith and boldness replace my spirit of fear
and insecurity.

Do a work in me that gives me hope in Jesus for Jesus, not for
blessings.

I pray for faith and peace instead of fear in finances.
I pray for hope and freedom instead of frustration over vocation.
I pray for waiting on the waters to part in Your timing.

I surrender ALL of this, ALL I have, and ALL I am into Your
hands. Amen.

PRAYER ABOUT VICTORY

Nothing that stands against me shall prosper. I am victorious
in Jesus, and through Him alone who died for my sins and
on the third day conquered death itself! Thank you, Jesus, for
overcoming the world. I place my trust in You. Amen.

Made in the USA
Monee, IL
01 March 2020

22547895R00098